dekalog

THE NEW HOME FOR SERIOUS FILM CRITICISM

The *Dekalog* series is a new list of publications, dedicated to presenting serious and insightful criticism on a wide range of subjects across the full spectrum of contemporary global cinema.

Each issue is a guest-edited specially-themed volume including the writings of a diverse collection of authors, from academic scholars and cultural theorists, film and media critics, and filmmakers and producers, to various personalities involved in all kinds of institutionalised cinephilia such as film festival directors, cinema programmers and film museum curators.

The intention, therefore, is to include the multiple voices of informed and complementary commentators on all things cinematic in dedicated volumes on subjects of real critical interest, especially those not usually served by established periodicals or book-length publications.

ALSO AVAILABLE IN THE *DEKALOG* SERIES:

Dekalog 1: On The Five Obstructions
guest edited by Mette Hjort

Dekalog 2: On Manoel de Oliveira
guest edited by Carolin Overhoff Ferreira

Dekalog 3: On Film Festivals
guest edited by Richard Porton

FORTHCOMING:

Dekalog 5: On Dogville
guest edited by Sara Fortuna & Laura Scuriatti

dekalog⁴
On East Asian Filmmakers

GUEST EDITOR: KATE E. TAYLOR

WALLFLOWER
LONDON & NEW YORK

First published in Great Britain in 2011 by
Wallflower Press
4 Eastern Terrace Mews
Brighton, BN2 1EP
www.wallflowerpress.co.uk

A catalogue record for this book is available from the British Library.

ISBN 978-1-906660-31-4 (pbk)
ISBN 978-0-231-50174-3 (e-book)
Printed in the United States.

Contents

Notes on Contributors

Saër Maty Bâ is Lecturer in Film Studies at the University of Portsmouth, UK). His current research is concerned with conceptualising film as archive and 'site' of memory, especially representations of genocide. His articles have appeared in *Studies in Documentary Film, Senses of Cinema, Film International* and *Cultural Studies Review*. He has also contributed chapters on ethnographic film, black masculinity and African Cinema; and currently is co-editor of two forthcoming projects: *The Encyclopedia of Global Human Migration* (Wiley-Blackwell) and *De-Westernizing Film Studies* (Routledge).

Colleen Berry is Associate Professor of Chinese Studies at the University of North Dakota, USA. Her primary research interests lie in the areas of Chinese film and modern Chinese literature. Recently, in addition to working on Chinese film comedy, she has been looking at the various Japanese and Chinese constructions of the historical figure, Kawashima Yoshiko/Chuandao Fangzi in film, literature, and other popular culture venues.

Masashi Ichiki is Professor of English and Multimedia Studies at the Graduate Institute of Human Science, Chikushi Jogakuen University, Fukuoka, Japan. His research interests include African American culture, media culture and representations of the past in film. His recent publications include, as co-editor, *Manga-wa Ekkyo suru* (2010) and a history of A-bomb manga in Japan in the *International journal of Asia and Pacific Studies*.

Barbara Jenni received her PhD in Chinese Studies from the University of Zürich, Switzerland; this focused on Chinese contemporary poetry and art and she has spoken at several international conferences on this topic.

Seung-hoon Jeong is Assistant Professor of Cinema Studies at New York University, Abu Dhabi. He has published extensively on a variety of topics including indexicality, cinematic ontology, Korean horror, and animals in film, as well as on filmmakers or theorists including André Bazin, Werner Herzog, Michael Haneke and Peter Greenaway.

E. K. Tan is Assistant Professor of Comparative Literary and Cultural Studies at the State University of New York at Stony Brook, USA. His areas of interest include Sinophone literature and film, modern and contemporary Chinese literature, Southeast Asian studies, Asian Diaspora studies, transnationalism and film theory. His recent publication includes a study of Hong Kong cinema and the portrayal of the Nanyang Chinese in the 1950s and 1960s in the *Journal of Chinese Cinemas*.

Xin Wang is Associate Professor of Chinese Studies at Baylor University, USA. He also serves as the director of the Asian Studies program at the university. His research and publications have been mainly focused on the civic culture of the emerging middle class in China and China's higher education reform. His recent research projects have focused on China's newly emerged urban art communities.

S. Louisa Wei is Associate Professor of Cinema Art and Cultural Studies at City University of Hong Kong. She is the co-author of *Women's Films: Dialogues with Chinese and Japanese Female Directors* (2009) and the producer and co-director of the historical documentary *Storm under the Sun* (2009). She has published many articles on women's cinema and female authorship in both English and Chinese.

Introduction:
On East Asian Filmmakers

Over the past few years there has been a steady rise in the focus on East Asian cinema. Big-budget Hollywood remakes, an increase in DVD availability and the success of directors and films at international festivals have all played their role in increasing the population of the cinema of this region. This volume of *Dekalog* is focused on the examination of a few selected directors who have all emerged from East Asia. The scope of the chapters is broad, including historical views, close film analysis, debates on globalisation and the dialogue between East and West in the work of the chosen directors. Broad also is the definition of 'East Asia' that we work from. For many, East Asian cinema is focused on Japan, South Korea and China; in this study we have engaged with a broader understanding which includes many of the smaller surrounding countries such as Thailand and Cambodia. With any investigation on such a wide topic there are always directors, and indeed countries, that are in danger of being missed from the list. For example there are no chapters specifically on world-famous directors such as Wong Kar Wai, Ang Lee, Kim Ki-duk, John Woo, Park Chan-wook or Lee Chang-dong. Whilst to many this may seem a serious oversight, the aim is to balance a review of more established directors such as Zhang Yimou and Jia Zhangke with consideration of important new voices such as Apichatpong Weerasethakul, as well as also offering a critical evaluation of less well known filmmakers such as Fang Xiogang and Ning Hao, and an overview of women working in the cinema of Japan and China. The key element was for the writers included here to engage with directors and films they found personally stimulating and central to their love of cinema. The writers themselves are from around the globe; many from East Asia, some from America, two from Europe and one from Africa, and this wide range of authors testifies to the increasing popularity, both academic and non-academic alike, of the cinema of the region. One of the key aims is also to ensure that the works are accessible to those from various academic backgrounds. The overviews offered by S. Louisa Wei and Xin Wang allow those from outside film studies to get an excellent overview of women directors and the career of Zhang Yimou respectively. The aims of these chapters are to spark new interests and pathways for further study and examination. The aim of this *Dekalog* edition is thus to offer something for everyone and to provide further points for discussion, debate and, of course, film viewing, for anyone interested in this fascinating and diverse region and its cinema.

We open with a short interview with acclaimed Japanese director Naomi Kawase. Kawase is unique as the only female director to have emerged from Japan who has achieved great acclaim on the international film circuit; 1997 saw *Moe no Suzaku* win the Caméra d'Or at the 50th Cannes Film Festival making Kawase the first Japanese, and the youngest ever, director to win this award. In this interview with S. Louisa Wei, Komatsu Ran and Yang Yuan-ying, Kawase speaks of the challenges and rewards which she has experienced as a woman filmmaker. Her work offers a highly personal approach to a variety of topics such as a disappearance of a child, an elderly parent suffering from Alzheimer's and the poverty of a small rural community, and Kawase's lyrical and melodic works can be seen to offer a direct challenge to those who still only focus on East Asia as the cinematic home of manga and kung-fu. As explored by S. Louisa Wei, she is part of a long, although often neglected, tradition of women filmmakers working in Japan and China. Wei's chapter, 'Women's Trajectories in Chinese and Japanese Cinemas: A Chronological Overview', is one of the first historical chartings of Japanese and Chinese women filmmakers in English. As Wei examines, many women directors have sought to challenge commonly held cultural and filmic structures and have, over the years, presented audiences with fiction film, action films, pornography and documentaries. The long-standing neglect of these filmmakers is something that will hopefully start to be challenged as the work of directors such as Naomi Kawase begins to gain more global attention.

It is not just women in East Asia who have been seeking to challenge cinematic structures and boundaries. One of the most notable directors carrying the 'sixth generation' tag, Jia Zhangke's films present the audience with themes of alienation, globalisation and the reality of youth culture in contemporary mainland China. In Jia's films there exists a constant interrogation of the notion of the 'authentic' and the 'real', making his film work a challenging addition to the cinematic canon. In her chapter 'Fusion Cinema: The Relationship Between Jia Zhangke's Films *Dong* and *Still Life*', Barbara Jenni examines Jia's work as a place where a meeting of different cinematic narratives and experiences occurs.

Fusion is an important concept in the examination of modern cinema as rapid globalisation takes place on an unprecedented scale. Media, business, politics, culture and sport have all played a role in the increasing interaction between East and West. Whilst directors such as Jia Zhangke offer a more intimate vision of modern China, films such as *Hero* (Zhang Yimou, 2002), *House of Flying Daggers* (Zhang Yimou, 2004) and *Red Cliff* (John Woo, 2008) have introduced Chinese cinema to a much wider and more populist international audience than ever before. The director *par excellence* at offering a vision of China that has succeeded on a global scale is Zhang Yimou. In his chapter 'From the Art House to the Mainstream: Artistry and Commercialism in Zhang Yimou's Filmmaking', Xin Wang charts the work of this remarkable director whose films have engaged critics and audiences alike for several decades and questions why and how his success has been so phenomenal.

In contrast to the big-budget extravaganzas that have come to mark the work of Zhang, J. Coleen Berry offers the lighter side of Chinese cinema. With an examination of two of the members of the 'new film comedy' genre: Fang Xiogang and Ning Hao, Berry charts why their works are significant in the study of Chinese cinema. She examines how their comedies appeal to large audiences and what they reveal about contemporary Chinese society and identity.

In the next chapter, E. K. Tan examines the relationship between cinema, memory and space through the work of Tsai Ming-liang. Born in Malaysia and working in Taiwan, Tsai's films offer a dialogue on how the 'postmodern global subject' has to struggle to re-establish human relations in a new world in which the emphasis on the global can often neglect the individual. Focusing on the films *The Hole* (1997) and *What Time is it There?* (2001) Tan considers the way in which Tsai examines how those displaced from the society around them seek alternative stories to narrate their lives and experiences.

Neglect is something that does not just happen inside the world of the film. In cinematic history, more 'populist' films have often been ignored or dismissed by critics and writers as unimportant to the cinematic canon. The success of Japanese cinema today can be seen as naturally germinating from earlier cinema and it is to the 1960s and 1970s that Masahi Ichiki takes us with his contribution on Kinji Fukasaku and the *Jinginaki Takahi* or *Battles without Honour or Humanity* series. Fukasaku, who is best known in the West for the hyper-violent *Battle Royale* (2000), begin filming in a turbulent era of Japanese history. After the end of World War II, debates on the way the Japanese economy and society were developing became more and more vocal and the violent, the controversial (as well as highly commercially poplar) *Jinginaki Takahi* series, focusing on the lives of Yakuza gangsters, offered a unique critique on the war and the legacy of the atomic bomb.

The legacy of violence is key in another of the directors that this volume examines. Cambodian director Rithy Pahn takes at the centre of several of his films the genocide that marked Cambodia during the reign of Pol Pot. In his in-depth and intricate study of Pahn, Saër Maty Bâ opens up questions of how film can be used to interrogate notions of past, present and future as it relates to memory as well as the search for the elusive 'real' in the legacy of forced migration and diaspora that has made contemporary Cambodia. This is perhaps not an article for the fainthearted but offers a stimulating and intriguing interrogation on the nature of film, documentation, memory and place.

The inclusion of Pahn and indeed the next director, Apichatpong Weerasethakul from Thailand, opens up the question of 'what is East Asia?' Is it an economic, a social, a political or a cultural space? Established economies such as Japan, Hong Kong, Taiwan and South Korea as well as the giant that is mainland China loom large in our consciousnesses but it is important to consider that the boundaries of this region stretch far and wide, and more and more cinema is coming from countries that we have hitherto heard relatively little from on the international film circuit. In his stimulating and highly personal review of Weerasethaku's main works, 'Black Hole in the Sky, Total Eclipse under the Ground: Apichatpong Weerasethakul and the Ontological Turn of Cinema', Seung-hoon Jeong introduces many of us to this remarkable director's work and its place in Thai as well as world cinema.

The increasing influence of East Asian cinema can be seen in the various Hollywood remakes that have taken place in the last decade. *The Ring* (2002), *The Departed* (2006), *Pulse* (2006) and *Shall we Dance* (2004), (*Ringu* (1998), *Internal Affaires* (2002), *Kairo* (2001) and *Shall We Dansu?* (1998) respectively), are just a few of the Hollywood films which are direct adaptations of Asian hits and went on to achieved success on the international market. Likewise, there has been an increase in the number of scholarly texts on the subject of East Asian cinema. Notable additions to the canon in the last couple of years alone include Darrell Davis and Emilie Yeh's (2008) extremely important focus on the industrial background and construction of the East Asian Film business. Via selected case studies, they offer an in-depth overview into how the East Asian industry is coping the current age of global financial pressure. Leon Hunt and Wing-Fai Leung (2008) offer an important examination of the interaction between the different cinemas in the East as well as the interplay between East and West. Kinnia Yau's work (2009, 2010) offers remarkable insights into how history, culture and film have interlinked over the last hundred years of East Asian cinematic development. The work of Aaron Gerow (2010), Denis Washburn and Carol Cavanaugh (2010), Isolde Standish (2011) and Catherine Russell (2008, 2011) has developed the English language writings on Japanese cinema. The previous small canon of work on South Korean cinema has grown with the addition of Darcy Paquet 's (2009), Jinhée Choi's (2010) and Kyung Hyun Kim's (2011) respective examinations of various aspects of this national cinema. Chinese-language cinema in particular has seen several important additions that include the work of Song Hwee Lim and Julian Ward (2011), Jason

McGrath (2010), Lingzhen Wang (2011) and Gary D. Rawnsley and Ming-Yeh T. Rawnsley's (2011) examination of Zhang Yimou's 2002 film *Hero* presents the most in-depth study of an individual Chinese film to date.

The role of film festivals has come under particular scrutiny. *Dekalog 3: On Film Festivals* (Porton 2009) and Ruby Cheung and Dina Iordonova's (2010) collected edition both examine the power and importance of film festivals (in both the West and in East Asia) and discuss how festivals operate as a tool for the dissemination, development and one of the main arenas where global economic and cultural success of East Asian cinema is negotiated.

Film festivals, however, are just one marker of success; the issues and problems that face East Asian directors are of course multiple. The recent economic crisis, political instability and the ever present influence of Hollywood is a constant challenge to those who wish to make and produce films. There is a tremendous pressure, both external and internal, on respective countries' film industries and directors often have to balance the need for box office success with the desire to make more challenging and artistic work. The relatively cheap availability of cameras, the internet, and advanced and easily accessibly digital technologies all add another dimension to contemporary filmmaking and how East Asian directors, both established and upcoming, adapt to the changes in the film industry is a continuous and fascinating question. What is clear is that many directors choose to face the challenges head on and hopefully continue to produce innovative and fascinated film work.

NOTE: In terms of name order we have for the most part kept to the traditional method of writing Japanese, Korean and Chinese names placing the surname first. However, where a Western-style name has been deliberately adopted (such as Jackie Chan, Bruce Lee and Naomi Kawase) we have used this to avoid confusion.

Bibliography

Choi, Jinhee (2010) *The South Korean Film Renaissance: Local Hitmakers Global Provocateurs*. Middletown: Wesleyan University Press.

Cheung, Ruby & Dina Iordanova (eds) (2010) *Film Festival Yearbook 3: Film Festivals and East Asia*. St Andrews: St Andrews Film Studies.

Davis, Darrell W. & Emilie Y. Yeh (2008) *East Asian Screen Industries*. London: BFI.

Gerow, Aaron (2010) *Visions of Japanese Modernity: Articulations of Cinema, Nation, and Spectatorship, 1895-1925*. Berkeley: University of California Press.

Hunt, Leon & Wing-Fai Leung (2008) *East Asian Cinemas: Exploring Transnational Connections on Film*. London: IB Tauris.

Kim, Kim Hyun (2011) *Virtual Hallyu: Korean Cinema of the Global Era*. Durham: Duke University Press.

Lim, Song Hwee & Julian Ward (2011) *The Chinese Cinema Book*. London: BFI.

McGrath, Jason (2010) *Postsocialist Modernity: Chinese Cinema, Literature, and Criticism in the Market Age*. Palo Alto: Stamford University Press.

Paquet, Darcy (2009) *New Korean Cinema: Breaking the Waves*. London: Wallflower Press.

Porten, Richard (ed.) (2009) *Dekalog 3: On Film Festivals*. London: Wallflower Press.

Rawnsley, Gary D. & Ming-Yeh T. Rawnsley (eds) (2011) *Global Chinese Cinema: The Culture and Politics of Hero*. London and New York: Routledge.

Russell, Catherine (2008) *The Cinema of Naruse Mikio*. Durham: Duke University Press.

_____ (2011) *Classical Japanese Cinema Revisited*. London and New York: Continuum Press.

Standish, Isolde (2011) *Politics, Porn and Protest: Japanese Avant-Garde Cinema in the 1960s and 1970s*. London and New York: Continuum Press.

Wang, Lingzhen (2011) *Chinese Women's Cinema: Transnational Contexts*. New York: Columbia University Press.

Washburn, Dennis & Carole Cavanaugh (2010) *Word and Image in Japanese Cinema*. Cambridge: Cambridge University Press.

Yau, Kinnia S. (2009) *Japanese and Hong Kong Film Industries: Understanding the Origins of East Asian Film Networks*. London and New York: Routledge.

_____ (2010) *Chinese-Japanese-Korean Cinemas: History, Society and Culture*, Hong Kong: Hong Kong University Press.

An Interview with Naomi Kawase

Interviewers: S. Louisa Wei, Komatsu Ran, and Yang Yuanying

Location: Kawase's Tokyo residence, August 2004;

translated by S. Louisa Wei

Q: Among younger Japanese film directors, you have received more international attention than most. We would like to know, when did you start to take an interest in filmmaking and have you been influenced by any particular film master?

A: I was born in Nara and grew up in the countryside. When I was little, no one around me ever thought about making a film, so neither did I. I was good at sports and didn't have a particular interest in arts. When I was in high school my height reached 1.67 metres. I became a member of the school basketball team and took part in the selection process of provincial team members. My dream then was to become an athlete. I took photographs during the sport meetings in school but did not pay much attention to the cinema club. I enjoyed team work in high school but did not have much chance for visual production as we were in the countryside. After graduation I still hoped to do something with friends.

My motivation for entering the visual media school was to improve my skills of photography for sport events. After I turned 18, I was able to use 8mm cameras and shot a lot of landscapes. Since then, I developed an interest in the moving image.

Q: What do you hope to express through moving images?

A: Life, everything about life, especially the joy of life. People, their thoughts and other invisible things about them.

Q: Have you encountered problems as a female director?

A: Not that much. In my school time, there was less discrimination against women. Shooting on location, the crew members thought it was interesting to work with women. They wouldn't let me do heavy labour. They took care of me because I am a woman director.

Q: Many film directors find the funding of their films to be the most frustrating issue in production. What is it like for you?

A: I feel that as long as I have a good script, there will be funding. After *Moe no suzaku* [1997] won an award, my financing became easier. When people believe in me, the funding becomes easier. After I wrote my scripts, a producer became interested and made an investment in my film. I feel that the producer and the director should be partners and understand one another. I wrote the script, but he had to pay for the production. I need to make the producer happy too.

Q: Do you think your work expresses your feminine experiences? Do you have reservations when expressing yourself?

A: I am a woman and I naturally see things from a woman's point of view. I can manage to see things from a man's point of view when I want to. When I express myself, I hope I can express a hundred per cent of what I feel.

Q: Do you have the audience in mind during your creative process?

A: I imagine myself to be the audience. I think about what I want to see, and then I will make the images. So you can also say I don't have a particular concern of the audience's need. I do care about the producer's thoughts, according to which I will make changes in my creative process. I don't belong to any film company, so I may lose the chance to make movies if I fail, even just once.

Q: Are you in touch with other female directors? Has your producer ever found your feminine consciousness to be a problem?

A: No. But they would say only women would shoot this way. Mostly, they are friendly though. Other female directors think their gender really matters, so we don't have much to talk about. I feel more films can be made by women though, especially in Japan.

Q: Your films have been to a lot of festivals, but how do Japanese audiences react to your films?

A: There is not much difference between Japanese and foreign audiences. People who understand my films like them. In Japan, people who love films would understand my films. Those people who only watch Hollywood films and TV dramas find my films difficult to understand. In foreign countries, it is the same. My films are certainly not for the masses or made in any genre. I do not have such motivation either. I only hope to express my thoughts. My films are only screened in single cinemas and never see a wide release. Even though I received an award at Cannes, there were not many people coming to watch my films in Japan. Without the awards, there would be even less people.

Q: What are some of your favourite films by other directors?

A: I like Victor Erice's *The Spirit of the Beehive*. His works were shown in Japan. I also liked Tsai Ming-liang's *The River*. It is an interesting film.

Filmography

Embracing (Ni tsutsumarete) (short), 1992. Dir. Naomi Kawase. Japan: Kumie.

Katatsumori (short), 1994. Dir. Naomi Kawase. Japan: Kumie.

Ten (Mitak) (short), 1995. Dir. Naomi Kawase. Japan: Kumie.

Moe no Suzaku (feature film), 1997. Dir. Naomi Kawase. Japan: Bandai Picture Company.

The Weald (documentary), 1998. Dir Naomi Kawase. Japan: Kumie.

Firefly (*Hotaru*) (feature film), 2000. Dir. Naomi Kawase. Japan: Dentsu Entertainment.

Sky, Wind, Fire, Water, Earth (*Kya Ka Ra Ba A*) (short), 2001. Dir. Naomi Kawase. Japan: Sento Inc.

Letter from a Yellow Cherry Blossom (*Tsuioku no dansu*), 2003. Dir. Naomi Kawase. Japan: Sento Inc.

Shara (*Sharasojyu*) (feature film), 2003. Dir. Naomi Kawase. Japan: Real Product.

Naissance et maternité (*Tarachime*) (documentary short), 2006. Dir. Naomi Kawase. Japan/France: Kumie, Arte France Cinéma.

The Mourning Forest (*Mogari no mori*) (feature film), 2007. Dir. Naomi Kawase. Japan/France: Kumie, Celluloid Dreams, Centre National de la Cinématographie.

Nanayomachi (feature film), 2008. Dir. Naomi Kawase. Japan/France: Digital Contents Trust, Kumie, Local Colour Films, Real Products.

In Between Days (documentary short), 2009. Dir. Naomi Kawase and Isaki Lacuesta. Spain/Japan: Centre de Cultura Contemporania de Barcelona, Departament de Cultura de la Generalitat de Catalunya, Kumie.

Visitors (segment 'Koma') (feature film), 2009. Dir. Naomi Kawase, Lav Diaz, Sang Soo-Hong. Japan/South Korea/Philippines: Kumie, Jeonju International Film Festival.

Genpin (Documentary), 2010. Dir. Naomi Kawase. Japan: Kumie.

Hanezu (*Hanezu no tsuki*) (feature film), 2011. Dir. Naomi Kawase. Japan: Kumie.

Women's Trajectories in Chinese and Japanese Cinemas: A Chronological Overview

S. Louisa Wei

Arguably, the existing writings on Chinese and Japanese cinemas share an obvious deficiency: female directors and their works are often overlooked as they do not readily or neatly fit into existing categories or trends of mainstream and art-house film studies. Whilst Western feminist theories have provoked fundamental re-examinations of 'her stories' in literary and visual discourses, substantial studies on female authorship and women's cinema in Chinese and Japanese contexts have only just begun.

Despite the academic neglect and industrial bias, women are clearly making films. Since 1985 the Tokyo International Women's Film Festival (TIWFF) has showcased around two hundred films by over thirty female directors from Japan, over twenty from Chinese-language territories and over a hundred from other countries. The organisers of the festival edited an anthology entitled *Films of the World Women Directors* (2001) and produced two documentaries, *Women Make Films: The Tokyo International Women's Film Festival* (2004) and *Viva, Women Directors* (2007), that respectively introduces 27 female filmmakers from Japan and twelve female directors from Asia and elsewhere. In China, the great achievements of female directors in the early 1980s, and especially in 1985, resulted in the 1986 'Forum on

Female Directors and Women's Cinema', an event attended by ten directors as well as film critics and scholars. The participants discussed such notions as the Chinese tradition of 'women-themed film' in comparison to Western concepts such as 'woman's film', 'feminist film' and 'women's cinema'. In 2009, *Women's Cinema: Dialogues with Chinese and Japanese Female Directors*, a book co-authored by Yang Yuanying and myself was published in Chinese. The book includes articles by seven Chinese female directors and 24 long interviews with fourteen female directors from mainland China, three from Hong Kong, one from Taiwan, six from Japan, as well as three TIWFF organiser/curators. In 2011 *Chinese Women's Cinema: Transnational Context* edited by Lingzhen Wang was published in English by Columbia University Press and brought together essays on the topic from both sides of the Pacific, and for the first time devoted discussions towards female auteurs and their film works within the transnational cultural discourse.

This essay attempts to present a very brief history from the mid-1920s to 2010 (literally focusing only on women directors and not their male counterparts), and aims to introduce important feature film directors from mainland China, Hong Kong, Taiwan and Japan. Since each of these four territories has its own filmic traditions and history, directors are introduced following the chronological order of their directorial debuts and are compared to their contemporaries from other regions. Due to length limitation this essay will mainly include female directors of fiction films and will offer an overview rather that in-depth analysis of the works. Of those directors who emerged since the 1980s, as a general rule only those who directed at least two features will be included. This study serves as one of the first English-language accounts of the historical trajectory of Chinese and Japanese female directors and will hopefully spark further debate and interest across the field.

Pioneer Female Directors: 1920s–1940s

During this period, female directors were very rare in any national cinema although Germaine Dulac (France, 1882–1942), Leni Riefenstahl (Germany, 1902–2003) and Dorothy Arzner (USA, 1897–1979) each received recognition in her own respective national cinemas as prominent female pioneers. Chinese film history maintains that Xie Caizhen (dates unknown) was the first female director from this region; she wrote and directed a silent film entitled *An Orphan's Cry* (1925), a family melodrama produced by the Nanxing Film Company. This film caused a huge sensation at the time, partly because it was directed by a woman and partly due to its very complicated plot. Nevertheless despite the film's success, details of Xie's career and life (before and after this release), have not yet been unearthed. Like many female directors she has disappeared from the cinematic canon and has been largely forgotten by history.

Another woman who directed films in the 1920s was Wang Hanlun (1903–78) (although no official film history includes her as a director despite her success as an actress). She became a top silent star after her first screen appearance in *Orphan Rescues Grandfather* (1923), a box-office hit that saved its production company from bankruptcy. Her films made the producers rich but she herself did not get paid; she won a lawsuit against the production company but all she received by way of compensation was a bad cheque. In 1929 she set up the Hanlun Film Company, bought famous scriptwriter Bao Tianxiao's screenplay for *The Revenge of an Actress* and invited a renowned director – Bu Wancang – to direct the film. As the director was suffering an emotional breakdown and spent a vast amount of time on the racetrack rather than the set, Wang Hanlun was forced to direct and edit the film herself: 'I bought the scene breakdown script with 800 yuan, and a projector. I played the film bit by bit at home and cut it bit by bit. After forty days, I finally succeeded' (Wang H. 1996: 7). She then took the film on tour and screened it in over a dozen cities. She made a fortune and left the film world in 1930. Her story reflects the difficulties women faced in the society at that time as well as the tremendous skills and commitment showed by those early women. It is telling of her personality that according to Wang Hanlun herself, her favorite role was Zhiruo in *The Abandoned Woman* (1924). After being abandoned by her husband who had a new love, Zhiruo manages to make a living on her own and participates in a woman's association. When her husband comes to take her back, she rejects him. He then sues her as an escaped wife. She dies while dreaming of a society where women have a say about their own fate.

The only woman directing Chinese-language films in the 1930s and

1940s was American-born Esther Eng (1914–70) who is regarded as the first female director to direct Chinese-language films in both the US and Hong Kong. Betty Cornelius (a.k.a. Betty Bowen), a journalist and keen advocate of women artists, wrote about Esther Eng in the *Seattle Times* of 9 June 1941: 'Still in her teens, with no background for such a venture, Esther went to Hollywood, rented a studio on Sunset Boulevard and made her first picture for Chinese markets here and in China.' Unpublished documents from the Shanghai Film Archive and various 1930s newspapers from Hong Kong also record this venture that resulted in a Sino-American production called *Iron Blood Fragrant Soul* (a.k.a *Heartaches*, 1935). In 1936, Esther Eng brought the film, together with its leading actress and her close friend Wai Kim Fong, to Hong Kong. The film was premiered at the Queens Theatre just in time to offer for a patriotic boost for a China where war with Japan was imminent (see Law & Bren 2004: 92).

After China entered into a war with Japan in 1937 she directed *National Heroine* (1937) featuring a female pilot who fights for her country. The success of the film encouraged Esther Eng to stay in Hong Kong where she made a 'social education drama' entitled *Ten Thousand Lovers* and a romantic tragedy *Storm of Envy*; both films were released in Hong Kong in 1938. In the same year, she also co-directed *Husband and Wife for One Night* with Leung Wai-man and Woo Peng. Thanks to her bold creativity and press interest (who wrote not only about her work but also her romance and conflicts with her actresses and other women), her films were highly successful. In 1939 she made an all-actress film entitled *Women's World*, which portrayed 36 women in different professions and related the conditions of their existence in society. This film was completed shortly before MGM's *Women* (1939), another all-actress film with a crew of 130 women (see Yu 1997: 207). Esther Eng left Hong Kong during the Japanese occupation and made *Golden Gate Girl* in 1941 in San Francisco. The film received a favorable review in *Variety* magazine on 28 May 1941 but further Hollywood success did not follow. She arrived in Hong Kong after World War II but failed to make another movie deal there.

Back in California by mid-1947 she made a new film, *The Blue Jade* (a.k.a. *The Fair Lady in the Blue Lagoon*), starring Fe Fe Lee, who, like Wai Kim Fong, was also a Cantonese opera actress. Both actresses starred in three films by Esther Eng and both formed a close relationship with her. Apart from *The Blue Jade*, Fe Fe Lee was also the female lead in two other Ester Eng films: *Back Street* (a.k.a. *Too Late for Springtime*, 1948) – about the relationship between a Chinese girl and an Chinese-American GI, and *Mad Fire Mad Love* (1949) – where she played the mixed-race young woman of a Chinese father and native Hawaiian mother. *Mad Fire Mad Love* was advertised as the first colour feature made in the Hawaiian Islands and its plot involved the forbidden love affair between a mixed-race woman and a Chinese sailor. Then, with a gap of over a decade, Esther Eng's last film credit was as the New York location director of Woo Peng's *Murder in New York Chinatown* (1961). The film's producer, Siu Yin Fei (1920–) was a leading film actress and a good friend of hers during her years in New York. During my interview with her in New York on March 24, 2011, she confirmed that Esther Eng directed all exterior scenes while Woo Peng all interior scenes of the thriller.

With ten films to her director's credit Esther Eng was a pioneer in many senses. She was the first woman to bring a feminist consciousness regarding equal rights for women and the concerns of American-Chinese's lives into her films. As early as the 1930s she attempted to represent cross-cultural and transnational themes in cinema. She was the first to make Chinese-language films in the US and the first Chinese woman to make sound films in Hollywood (see Law & Bren 2003). And yet her work and the work of nearly all other early female directors are notably missing from the film history canon. Todd MacCarthy, a former critic of *Variety*, wrote about his complete astonishment when he discovered Esther Eng's *Golden Gate Girl* while reading through *Variety*'s back issues, calling her 'one filmmaker [who] has utterly eluded the radar of even the most diligent feminist historians and Sinophiles'. It is telling that despite being such an important filmmaker, *Variety* did not report further news of Esther Eng after the May 1941 review of *Golden Gate Girl* until her obituary appeared in January 1970 when she died of cancer at the age of 55 (see McCarthy 1995).

Shortly before the Sino-Japanese War, Kyoto-born Sakane Tazuko (1904–75), the former assistant director of Mizoguchi Kenji, debuted as a director with a film entitled *New Year Finery* (a.k.a. *First Image*, 1936). She wrote the following in that year: 'I want to portray the true figure of women seen from the realm of women with a thoroughness combined with my own view of life' (see Masumoto 2004: 247). During the production of the film, however, Sakane's crewmembers fiercely rejected her on the grounds of her gender. Even though she finally managed to deliver the completed film it was a critical and box-office failure (see Masumoto 2004: 249) and Sakane was never to direct another feature film. She went to Japanese-occupied Manchuria and became a director of non-fictional films for the Manchuria Film Association (the Japanese colonial production unit in Manchuria). She directed about ten 'cultural' films in Manchuria, which were usually one or two reels in length. The only film by her that survives today is *A Settler's Bride* (1943). When Sakane returned to Japan after the war, she could not even find a position as an assistant director, and worked as a script coordinator and editor for the rest of her career (see Kumagai 2004).

Chen Bo'er (1910–51), an actress who starred in left-wing stage dramas and films and was most famous for her role in *Fate of Graduates* (a.k.a. *Plunder of Peach and Plum*, 1934), was perhaps the only Chinese woman working as a director-producer in the 1940s. An activist during the Sino-Japanese War, Chen entertained Chinese soldiers with stage drama performances and went to the Communist base in Yan'an in 1940. There, she took part in writing plays and film scripts and coordinated the shooting of the famous documentary *Defending Yan'an* (1947). In 1946, she helped to establish the Northeast Film Studio that was reformed from the former Manchuria Film Association. There she produced seventeen episodes of newsreels on the 'Democratic Northeast' in 1947. One of the episodes, entitled 'Dream of the Emperor', which she wrote and directed, was the first puppet film of China (literally films made using puppets). Besides producing films, Chen also played an important role in the Central Film Bureau that worked to strengthen the link between her film work and her political ideology.

Post-war Women Directors: 1950s–1962

Seventeen years after Sakane Tazuko directed her first and only feature, Tanaka Kinuyo (1910–77), a top star from the silent film period, made her directorial debut with *Love Letter* (1953). Tanaka's film focuses on a male hero who writes love letters for Japanese wives left behind by American soldiers. When commenting on the challenge of taking up the director's role at the age of 43, she said in an interview: 'It was really a matter of knowing no fear'; after being treated like a star for decades, 'it was human skills [that she] needed more than technique' (in Masumoto 2004: 249). Tanaka's directorial debut received a vast amount of media attention thanks to both her status as 'star' and the film's subject matter. Post-war Japan had only just been released from the American occupation that had followed the country's defeat in World War II, and the tale of women abandoned by amorous Americans struck a chord. She continued to work as an actress and directed five more films between 1955 and 1961 including *The Moon Has Risen* (1955), *The Eternal Breasts* (1955), *The Wandering Princess* (1960), *Girls of Dark* (1961) and *Love Under the Crucifix* (1962). Criticism related to Tanaka's work shows that far from just imitating the prominent male directors that she had worked with as an actress, Tanaka constructed her own specific style of film directing. In Japan, her efforts presented a powerful challenge to the idea that women would be incapable of directing films and the previous dismissal of Tanaka as only an actor was remedied. Indeed, in recognition of her skills, Tanaka was the only woman who held membership of the Directors Guild of Japan until her death in 1977 (see Masumoto 2004: 253).

The lack of a consolidated charting of women making films in Japan resulted in Tanaka being mistakenly called the first woman director of Japan. This mistake has resulted in the ignorance of Sakane Tazuko's work for nearly seven decades. The different fates of Sakane and Tanaka reflect the deep-rooted discrimination against women in Japanese society and the film industry in particular. Without her star power and persistence, even Tanaka would have struggled as a female director working in the male oriented film industry.

The Japanese occupation of Taiwan ended in 1945 with the conclusions of World War II, and native Taiwanese cinema finally began to boom. At the time, films made in Shanghai were brought to Taiwan and achieved great success. China's Civil War was ended in 1949 after which the Communist government took over mainland China and the Nationalist government moved to Taiwan with a significant amount of capital and a wide group of cultural intellectuals. A large number of Shanghai-based filmmakers moved to Hong Kong and continued to make Mandarin-language films until the 1970s, when Cantonese cinema finally gained an upper hand. Among the

1950s new immigrants to Hong Kong, Malaysian-born actress Chen Juanjuan (1928–67) – 'China's Shirley Temple' – and famous director Ren Pengnian's daughter Ren Yizhi would eventually become film directors. At this point, Chinese-language cinema split into three separate streams of development in terms of language (Cantonese, Mandarin and/or Taiwanese) and geographical/cultural location (Hong Kong, mainland China and Taiwan).

In Hong Kong, Ren Yizhi (unknown–1979) worked first as an actress and then as a scriptwriter. Between 1955 and 1959 she co-directed eight films, mostly urban melodramas or light comedy, with other more famous male directors. In the 1960s she independently directed three films about love and marriage: *An Unfulfilled Wish* (1960), *Ah, It's Spring!* (1961) and *The Four Daughters* (1963). She was the first local female director to work in Hong Kong and continued to be the only woman actively directing films from the 1950s to the early 1960s. According to the Hong Kong Film Archive records, her films in this period were all black and white and mostly produced by Great Wall and Phoenix Film Companies. In 1972 she co-directed her last, and only colour, film, *Three Seventeen-Year-Olds* with Chen Juanjuan (who also co-directed four films with other male directors in the 1960s). Many of these films and the women that made them have been lost to time and more work will need to be done to uncover the works of these forgotten female directors.

In 1957 the female boss of Taipei's San Chong Ming Theatre, Chen Wenmin, decided to invest in a self-penned romance film entitled *Xue Rengui and Liu Jinhua*. Even though she had received no formal training, Chen managed to storyboard and present the film to a producer and secured the relatively well-known director Shao Luohui. After a disagreement however, Shao Luohui dropped the project and Chen Wenmin finished the production on her own. In the end, Shao Luohui was still credited as the director and herself (with the name Chen Fen) as the writer. This act of modesty has no official reasons but the need to have a well-known male director's name attached to the project may well have been key in this decision. (This story is similar to the case of *Revenge of an Actress* nearly twenty years earlier, where Wan Hanlun also kept Bu Wancang's name as the director though she did the job herself.) In 1958, Chen Wenmin wrote and directed a highly romantic film *Lost Bird* (1958), which was followed by five films in the romance genre. She seemed able to understand the needs and desires of her audience and all of her films did well at the box-office. In 1962, (shortly after Esther Eng made her last film), Chen Wenmin co-directed *The Second Spring* with Lin Fudi and retired from the film industry at the peak of Taiwanese-dialect film's decline. Given that her last film was in 1962 it is a sad reflection on the state of female filmmaking in Taiwan that so far no female director in Taiwan has surpassed her in terms of commercial success (see Huang 1994: 43).

In mainland China, former stage and film actress Wang Ping (1916–90), together with three other women – Wang Shaoyan (1924–), Dong Kena (1930–) and Wu Guoying (dates unknown) – was appointed as a film director at the August First Film Studio (a unit under the People's Liberation Army that specialised in war films). Wang Ping's earlier works, including *The Story of Liubao Village* (1957), foregrounding the love between a young soldier and a country girl, and *The Everlasting Radio Signals* (1958), about a former Red Army soldier's working in radio espionage, were great hits of the time. These films not only demonstrate her artistic maturity and personal style, but also more importantly set up a sexual/textual prototype for the 'revolutionary/war genre', which would continue to be the most prominent genre in mainland Chinese cinema all the way until the 1970s. As Yang Yuanying points out, 'The lovers or couples' relationship is one between a leader and a follower. They meet in a specific historical time and space and develop an unchangeable love while fighting for their ideals. For them, the battlefield is the field of love, while revolution equates to love' (1996: 31). In Wang Ping's films, the leader is always male but in contrast to the often male-led narratives, the various female characters' personal growth is vividly portrayed with convincing details. Many of the details were drawn from the director's own personal experiences linking her films closely to feminist ideals of film representing a female imagination and consciousness (see Johnston 1975). Wang Ping made thirteen features in her lifetime including two musical eulogies for Chinese Communist revolutionary history, *The East is Red* (1965) and *Songs of Chinese Revolution* (1990), however her most influential works were all made in the 1950s and 1960s. Due to her high rank in People's Liberation Army of China, she was often called a 'General Director', a title reflecting both her cultural status and a political prominence that few women director have achieved.

New Voices and Experiments: 1960s–1970s

It is a curious coincident that Esther Eng, Chen Wenmin and Tanaka Kinuyo all made their last film in 1962 as if announcing the end of a generation. Around the same time, two female colleagues of Wang Ping in the August First Film Studio, Dong Kena and Wang Shaoyan, directed their first films in the early 1960s. Unlike Wang Ping's work, Dong Kena's *A Grass on the Kunlun Mountain* (1962) reveals a strong sense of 'feminine consciousness' (focusing on the experiences and emotions of women) that at the time was comparatively rare. The believable and psychologically complex characters that Dong Kena created resulted in over a thousand letters from viewers crediting her with presenting women that they could all emotionally engage with. Compared to Wang Ping's heroines, Dong's female protagonists are more independent, never belonging to any man or finding their 'way' under man's direction. The enthusiastic audience response indicated that many audience members revelled in this comparatively liberated approach to represented modern Chinese womanhood. Dong Kena would eventually have sixteen films to her name making her one of the most prolific female directors in mainland China. Wang Shaoyan's most successful film was a revolutionary musical titled *Red Coral* (1961) and whilst its box-office success has ensured her remembrance in Chinese film cannons she remains unknown in the wider film circles.

Elsewhere in China women were also making their presence felt. In 1965, Yan Bili's (unknown–) film *Little Football* made her the first female director to work in Shanghai since 1949. Not long after, however, the chaotic decade of the Cultural Revolution (1966–76) resulted in the almost complete stagnation of mainland Chinese filmmaking. The directing careers of Yan Bili, Dong Kena, Wang Ping and Wang Shaoyan, like that of other older generation directors, were interrupted and not able to resume (if they ever did) until the early 1980s.

In Taiwan, since the film industry was influenced by the Japanese system of master/apprentice, women had little chance to enter the business (men did not hire women to be their apprentice and this was the only way one could gain entry). The early success of Chen Wenmin was exceptional and came about because she was in the position to fund her own productions.

For many women, the path to directing was one that developed from acting or writing. In 1961 Wang Man-jiao (1943–), an art college student and a finalist at the Miss China Beauty Pageant in 1960, was recommended to renowned director Li Shing who at the time was looking for an actress who could speak both Mandarin and Taiwanese. She would star in about 26 films before moving to television productions in the early 1990s. As Wang showed a talent for writing, she began to write screenplays in 1965 and wrote eight scripts that made it into production. She won the Best Script Award at the Taiwanese Dialect Film Exhibition in 1965 and proceeded to write three film scripts that same year. In 1966 she had a chance to direct a comedy entitled *A Short Man's Tour in Taiwan* (a.k.a. *Adventure of a Cloth Seller*), which was first screened on 1 July 1967. Wang Man-jiao was not only responsible for directing but also for sound and editing. This workload, combined with facing the pressure of the aggressive film market, unfortunately led to her decision to give up directing after only one feature (see Ye 1996: 233–6).

The situation in 1960s Japan was no better than that in Taiwan. After Tanaka Kinuyo, women practically disappeared from the director's chair for over a decade. In 1968, twenty-year-old Hamano Sachi (1948–) came to Tokyo with dreams of becoming a film director. She found her dreams destroyed since film studios would only hire young men with a university degree. She entered the soft porn film industry in hope that she could make 'real' movies later on. In 1970 she directed her first 'pink movie', about a seventeen-year-old girl who chooses her own sexual partners to learn about sex (see Yang and Wei 2009: 416). Hamano remained the only female director in the porn film industry for ten years before two former porn actresses began to direct: Tama Rumi (1949–) in 1981 and Yoshiyuki Yumi (1965–) in 1999. In 1984 Hamano Sachi founded her own independent company and continues to produce porn films from a women's point of view and to bring pleasure to a female audience. She is the most prolific among the three main female 'pink film' directors and has more than three hundred films to her director's credit.

A forgotten but significant female voice from the 1960s and 1970s Japan is Idemitsu Mako (1940–). Dreaming of becoming a writer she instead became a housewife whilst living in the US with her American painter husband. With two children to care for, she wandered into a camera shop one

day, bought a camera and began shooting short films (including one recording for Judy Chicago's 'Women's House' in 1972 (see Yang and Wei 2009:
408)). She returned to Japan and under the influence of the limited feminist
movement that was growing at the time, she continued her experimental
film, video and multimedia work from the 1970s all the way through to the
1990s. Even though she never made a feature film, she represents one of the
most important feminist voices in Japan, albeit an often-neglected one.

During the early 1970s three more female directors emerged in Hong
Kong but alas, they were soon forgotten. Gao Baoshu (1932–), a 1950s
immigrant to Hong Kong, first worked as an actress in dozens of films. In
1971 she set up the Baoshu Film Company with her husband and began
directing and producing. She directed *Human Traffic* (1974) and *Low Society*
(1976) which were only moderately successful. She retired from her film
career in the early 1980s. Yu Fengzhi directed her debut work *The First
Time* (1983) after producing several films. Meanwhile, Tang Shu-shuen
(1941–), who was born in mainland China, moved to Taiwan at the age of
sixteen and studied filmmaking in University of Southern California, left
a clearer mark on Hong Kong film history with four feature films to her
credit. Her debut *The Arc* (1970) tells the story of a widow and her daughter falling for the same man. Tang deals with 'a woman's inner emotional
life', and gained international recognition for 'a slowly paced eroticism
… filtered through a modern temperament' (Law 2001: 35) and is now
considered very much ahead of her time. Her second film *China Behind*
(1974), was shot in Taiwan with government support, and depicts a few
young mainlanders' escape to Hong Kong during the Cultural Revolution. It needs to be noted that 'escaping stories' have only come to the mass
media's attention recently making Tang Shu-sheun very prescient in her
choice of subject matter. The film was never shown in any Chinese-language territory and was seen at only a few international film festivals. Her
last two films were *Sup San Bup Dap* (1975) and *Hong Kong Tycoon* (1979),
both made in Cantonese. Hong Kong film scholar and independent director Yau Ching has written the first scholarly work that examines Tang
Shu-shuen's works in depth (2004). Yau praises Tang's last two films and
rebuffs the views of critics in Hong Kong at the time that had indirectly
ended Tang Shu-shuen's film career.

First Golden Era: 1977–1983

In 1977, the year of Tanaka Kinuyo's death and fifteen years after her last film, Hidari Sachiko (1930–2001), another famous Japanese actress who had won several international awards, directed her first and only work, *The Far Road*. The film depicted the building of the Japan National Railway from the point of view of the workers' wives. The film 'realistically chronicled the travails of working-class women' and offers a portrayal of women 'historically rare in Japanese film' (Brennen 1998). Joan Mellen also published her review of twelve films about post-war Japan in the *New York Times Review* on 22 April 1979, stating that 'Miss Hidari's film deprives us of any illusion about this recourse [to create labour unions] for the besieged Japanese citizen'. Sachiko's success did not however pave the way for her to make another feature film or to enhance the overall status of women directors in Japan.

Nevertheless, during the 1980s women in Japan enjoyed reasonable success. In 1980, Kurisaki Midori (1937–) a formal actress of the Daie Film Studio, directed a film entitled *Dark Hair*, a fifty-minute film about the significance of black hair in the Japanese conception of beauty and femininity. The following year, she directed a puppet film called *The Love Suicides at Sonezaki* (1981) that was shown in film festivals in Europe to great acclaim.

In Taiwan the 'Healthy Realism' film trend promoted by the Taiwanese government in the 1960s and 1970s was replaced by a wave of romantic films, in which the most prolific female director of Taiwan so far, Liu Lili (1938–), emerged. Liu began her film career as log-keeper and assistant director in 1963 and directed her first film in 1977. She directed nine films adapted from bestselling romances by Qiong Yao between 1979 and 1983 and continued to direct similar television dramas, also from Qiong's works, until the early 1990s. These films were all produced by the company owned by Qiong Yao's husband, Grand Star Film Enterprise, and mostly starred Brigitte Lin and Chin Han who were the top box-office duo at the time. As Lu Feiyi points out, the romance genre does not help 'the establishment of the feminine consciousness, but provides an exit for the spiritual boredom' (1998: 134). Such a film genre not only 'resolves social anxiety, consoles women's lonely hearts', but also strengthens 'the identification with nation and the traditional order of the patriarchal society' (*Ibid.*). Although the genre itself was often neglected as trite and formulaic, its 'contribution to the groups with vested interests was a lot more than the official renaissance movement' (*Ibid.*: 135). For many, the romances of Qiong Yao are as socially and culturally relevant as the more political celluloid that would later be produced by movements such as the Taiwanese New Wave.

After 1980 the emergence of the Taiwanese New Wave saw 'social realist films' become the mainstream of Mandarin-language films. Films around this time tended to portray sex, violence, gambling, gangs and underground societies and the focus was on the underbelly of modern Taiwan. Around this time a sub-stream of films that featured 'revenge-seeking girls' appeared. Female director Yang Chia-yun (1947–), who first established herself as a romance director with *Morning Mist* (1978) and *Love Comes from the Sea* (1980), began to represent unconventional female roles from her third film *The Unsinkable Miss Calabash* (1981) onwards. This was followed by 'revenge girl' stories like *Who Dares Challenge Me* (1981), *The Lady Avenger* (1981) and *Exposed to Danger* (1982) and all focused on bullied and marginalised women seeking revenge. Yang's next production *Crazy Girl Camp* (1981) combined comedy and the 'campus film' genre and features girls in skimpy clothing whose primary objects are men. They always finish off the 'male devils' after having a good laugh at them. Although these were not part of an overtly feminist movement, Yang Chia-yun's films show an attempt to frame a new vision of women as active narrative participants who were capable of aggression in their own defense. In her last feature film *Women Warriors of Kingmen* (1983), she turned to the writing of 'women's history' which is a project that is continued in her 1998 award-winning documentary *A Secret Buried for 50 Years: A Story of Taiwanese 'Comfort Women'*.

Also in Taiwan in the early 1980s, Li Mei-mi (1946–) presented *Unmarried Mother* (1980), which focused on the hotly debated issue of unmarried motherhood. She directed another film entitled *Girl's School* (1982) which boldly explored the issue of homosexuality amongst the young.

The Hong Kong New Wave took place from 1979 to the early 1980s and Ann Hui (1947–) was an important figure. Her early works include *The Secret* (1979), *The Spooky Bunch* (1980), *The Story of Woo Viet* (1981) and *Boat People* (1982) and not only established her fame as both a commercially successful director with serious political concerns, but her films have become known as New Wave 'classics'. She would become one of Hong Kong's most prolific directors and her works all touch on a few thematic threads that have continued to appear throughout her career; namely the use of horror (*The Secret* and *The Spooky Bunch*), a focus on questions of immigration and marginalisation (*The Story of Woo Viet* and *Boat People*) and the loves and fates of ordinary women.

Like Ann Hui, Mabel Cheung (1950–) studied cinema overseas before returning to Hong Kong. Her first three works, *Illegal Immigrant* (1985), *An Autumn's Tale* (1987) and *Eight Tales of Gold* (1989), became part of what is now called her 'migration trilogy'. In 1997, she made *The Soong Sisters*, charting the lives of Charlie Soong's three daughters who went to college in the US and married three of the most prominent men of China's modern history. This film was the high point of Cheung's career and was also the biggest box-office hit among all her films. *The Soong Sisters* premiered at the Tokyo International Women's Film Festival and then went on to tour in Japan, where it still maintains the position of top-grossing film at the Iwanami Theatre (an art cinema which specialises in the screening of women's cinema and political works).

Florence Yu has five films to her director's credit (two of these are co-directed with her husband Yang Qun (1935–)). Her independent directions are *Morning Goodbye* (1973), *Disco Fever* (1979) and *First Time* (1983). She would continue to work in the producer's capacity into the 1990s. Rachel Zen (1951–), who first became noticeable for her 'Under Lion Mountain' television series (similar to Ann Hui's career which also began in television), would eventually join Ann Hui in the classification of 'New Wave director'. Her feature films, *Cream, Soda and Milk* (1981), *Love Bittersweet* (1984) and *Life Goes On* (1989), are mainly about family and love. Column writer and television drama director Wu Xiaoyun made *Rainbow Clouds* (1982), a film about three boys and three girls, which attracted some attention at the time.

After collaborating with two female directors in a three-part film entitled *Oil* (1979), Angel Mak (unknown-) continued to make horror thriller *The Siamese Twins* (1984) and *Parking Service* (1986) for the Shaw's Company. Another female director Angie Chen studied cinema in the US and returned to Hong Kong in the early 1980s. She soon got a chance to directed *Maybe It's Love* (1984) that was followed by *My Name Ain't Susie* (1985) telling the story of a bar hostess set in the 1950s and 1960s Waichai (a district frequented by foreign sailors and soldiers). The next year she directed another film entitled *Chaos by Design* (1986). Over twenty years later she directed *This Darling Life* (2008), a story based her dog's death, and is now completing a documentary on American-Chinese writer Nie Hualing. Angie Chan's films often depict close relationships that exist between women (often with an undercurrent of lesbianism). Unfortunately, however, many women who directed films in the 1990s would only go on to make one feature film and would quickly disappear from the film world. Finding funding for films, difficult in most cases, would prove to be impossible for many women directors.

First Waves of Women's Cinema: 1984–1992

From the 1980s Japanese women had more chances to direct than ever before; however, many of their directorial careers were very short lived. In 1981 renowned female photographer Yoshida Ruiko (1938–) directed a Toho-produced film, *Long Run*, focusing on a Japanese skater in America. Writer Takahashi Yoko filmed her novel *I Like Rain* (1983); actress Watanabe Eriko (1955–) directed *Bastard, I Am Angry* (1988); Shiina Sakurako directed a biography entitled *Family Dance* (1988); and actress Momoi Kaori released *Moments in Our Life* (1991). These directors rarely made more than one film and these films are often largely personal and based on their own experiences. The most important female director who emerged in the 1980s and has continued her career into present is perhaps Makitsubo Tatsuko (1940–), who set up her independent film company PAO in 1985 and made an educational trilogy under the title of *Message of Life and Love*, which includes *To Children* (1986), *Young People* (1987) and *Children of the Earth* (1993). In 1998 she made a film entitled *I Like Myself* that explored the various traumas that face teenage girls. After 2000 she made two touching films concerning the care of the elderly: *Old Parents* (2000) and *Where Mom Is* (2003). These films seek to link social and familiar problems and aim to address the wider cultural implications of the issues concerned.

A notable woman director who emerged in Taiwan in the late 1980s was Huang Yu-shan (1954–) who worked as an assistant director for veteran director Li Shing between 1977 and 1979 before studying film in the US. In 1982, returning to Taiwan with a Master's degree from New York University, she began to make documentaries. Her feature films include *Autumn Tempest* (1988), *Twin Bracelets* (1989), *Peony Bird* (1990), *Wild Love* (1999), *Story of Eastern Pond* (2005) and *The Song of Chatain Mountain* (2007). *Twin Bracelets* was shown at international film festivals and this enabled Huang to have in-depth discussions with various American independent filmmakers and feminist directors. From then on she began to consciously push forward films about women and to organise women's film shows and festivals together with encouraging independent film/video productions by Taiwanese women. Huang Yu-shan remains an important voice in Taiwanese women's cinema and her works are long overdue a retrospective.

In mainland China between 1979 and 1989 (according to an incomplete survey), '59 female directors made a total of 182 films' (Yang 1996: 17). This comparatively large number is in part thanks to the fact that from the 1950s to the 1960s, at the Beijing Film Academy and Central Theatre Academy, there was a policy to admit twenty per cent female students into the directing department (primarily for the benefit of acting classes rather than to encourage female directors per se). Although the Cultural Revolution had nearly stopped all film production between 1966 and 1974, by 1979 more than fifty female graduates from the two academies were assigned jobs in major studios and many would soon become directors. Wang Hao-wei (1940–), Zhang Nuanxin (1940–), Huang Shuqin (1939–), Shi Shujun (1939–), Wang Junzheng (1945–) and Lu Xiaoya (1941–) are among the best-known female directors of the 'Fourth Generation'. This generation is the first generation of women who benefited from the stated communist goal of equality for all. Many aimed to 'hold up half of the sky'; however, many would have to tread the thin line of balancing family and work and their careers never achieved the success of their male counterparts. Since 1984 an even younger generation of female directors (who were classmates of the so-called 'fifth-generation' directors) also began to direct. By the end of the 1980s, Hu Mei (1958–), Peng Xiaolian (1953–), Li Shaohong (1955–), Liu Miaomiao (1962–) and Ning Ying (1958–) had all established themselves with several impressive film works.

From the mid-1980s to the early 1990s there was a wave of women's cinema presenting 'unusual' (or 'truthful', depending on one's point of view) images of women on the Chinese screen. In this wave of films women's roles in society and their choices in life are redefined; women's desires and experiences are explored and women's visions and voices are expressed to a level not previously achieved. What is truly remarkable is that female directors of three generations all took a part in this wave; it was not only a film movement for the younger generation.

Women's films with a clear notion of feminine consciousness and a distinct female authorship style finally emerged. Hu Mei's *Army Nurse* (1984) was notable for being regarded by American feminist film scholar E. Ann Kaplan as the first Chinese film to clearly express woman's sexual desire (see 1985: 42). Zhang Nuanxin's *Sacrificed Youth* (1986) focuses on the chaotic years of the Cultural Revolution during which a Chinese girl in her standard Communist Lenin suit (a plain and practical outfit popular with communist party members) is sent down to the countryside for 're-education'. When the local girls regard her as 'ugly' she learns that the 'civilisation' that she comes from has eliminated her rights to pursue beauty and to desire love and affection. Liu Miaomiao's *Women on the Long March* (1987) fills in the blanks in the history of the Communist Revolution with a close look at a detachment of young girls and women in the Red Army who were left alone by the main troops before the Long March. The cinematic representation is both shocking and touching and covers a period of history and events that many would rather forget. Huang Shuqin's *Women Demon Human* (1988) describes the coming-of-age story of a Chinese opera actress who is famous for her male impersonation. At every stage of her development her gender always creates an obstacle for her. Peng Xiaolian's *Women's Story* (1989) follows three countrywomen's adventure to the city. All facing difficult situations at home, they choose instead to challenge authority and change their fates rather than to endure unhappy lives and marriages like their mothers. Wang Junzheng's *Woman, Taxi, Woman* (1994) focuses on the unlikely friendship between a Master's-level student who falls in love with her married professor and a taxi driver who belongs to the pro-democratic Chinese 'grass roots movement'. Li Shaohong's *Blush* (1994) fills in another blank in Chinese history by deconstructing the 'official' record of women as a unified communist voice. In her representation of the Communist reform of prostitution systems Shaohong focuses on the everyday hardships faced by the women.

As the state-owned film industry underwent reform around 1993 film producers and investors became focused only on financial return. As a result many women filmmakers born in the 1930s and 1940s were out of a job. The production of films by female directors nearly came to a standstill between 1995 and 2000. During this difficult period, however, two unlikely films appeared, directed by women focusing on female narratives and experiences. *The Sun Bird* (1997) was directed by one of the most famous dancers in China, Yang Liping (1959–). The film is based on her real-life story and reflects her memories of childhood in a primitive rural village and later experiences in the modern city. The film's three interlaced levels of narrative each focuses on a different aspect of feminine representation: while the 'present reality' is seen through the famous dancer who has an eye problem, the 'past memory' is presented in the dancer's childhood experience of her gender, and the level caught 'in-between' utilises the language of the female body in dance. The other very notable film from this period was directed by American-Chinese actress Joan Chen (1962–). *Xiu Xiu: Story of a Sent-down Girl* (1998) is adapted from writer Yan Geling's novella and depicts the desperation of urban youth 'sent down' to a rural area by Chairman Mao Zedong during the Cultural Revolution. The protagonist innocently believes that she needs to sleep with a string of men to get permission to go back to the city but all the men simply take advantage of her and abandon her to her fate.

The Independent Age: 1990–2000s

Although both in mainland China and Hong Kong film studios declined in the 1990s, female directors in Hong Kong seemed to be less affected than their mainland peers and simply continued on working despite the economic downturn. The most important female director who emerged a decade after Ann Hui and Mabel Cheung in Hong Kong is perhaps Macau-born Clara Law (1957–). She began directing in 1990 and would soon be considered an important director of Hong Kong's Second New Wave together with directors such as Stanley Kwan and Wong Kar-Wai. Like both male directors' works before 1997, Clara Law's films reveal a serious concern for Hong Kong's cultural-political identity. *Farewell China* (1990) focuses on a Chinese couple's migration to the US and ends with the woman's madness after living in New York for several years without her husband and son. *Autumn Moon* (1992) presents a girl waiting for her grandmother's death so she can join her family that has migrated from Hong Kong to Canada. The girl forms an unexpected friendship with a young Japanese man who is looking for the most 'authentic' Chinese cuisine, something he eventually finds in the grandmother's kitchen. Law herself also relocated to Australia around 1997 and made *Floating Life* (1996) about a family from Hong Kong. her next film, *The Goddess of 1967* (2000), is about a young Japanese man's unexpected journey with a blind girl. In 2010, after not making a narrative feature for a decade, she came back to Chinese-language cinema circles with *Like a Dream*, which presents the pursuit of true love through time and space and laments the loss of tradition and memory during the process of urban modernisation.

Ann Hui made more films in the 1990s, many taking on themes which appeared in earlier works to a new level. The moderate horror in early thrillers like *The Secret* and *The Spooky Bunch* was elaborated in *Visible Secret* (2001) reflecting the abyss of psychological illness. The concern over new immigrants and other marginalised people seen in *The Story of Woo Viet* and *Boat People* have been varied and enriched in *Song of Exile* (1990), *Ordinary Heroes* (1998) and *Night and Fog* (2009). The loves and fates of women are portrayed in *Love in a Fallen City* (1984), *Song of Exile*, *Summer Snow* (1994), *The Stunt Woman* (1996), *Eighteen Springs* (1997), *Jade Goddess of Mercy* (2003), *The Postmodern Life of My Aunt* (2006), *The Way We Are* (2008) and *A Simple Life* (2011). These themes often overlay in her films that involve a conscious writing of the reality and lives of ordinary people and focus especially on women's history as part of Hong Kong's collective past.

Mabel Cheung's 1998 film *City of Glass* is a beautiful reminiscing of Hong Kong's history from the 1960s through to 1997 (although very different in tone compared to Ann Hui's *Ordinary Heroes* which examines a similar topic). Her last feature film was *Beijing Rocks* (2001) exploring the underground rock scene. Her most recent production, in which she worked as producer, is the very touching *Echoes of the Rainbow* (2010). Interestingly, this is the 'come-back' work of Cheung and her husband Alex Law who have worked closely throughout their respective film careers.

In Taiwan Wang Siu-di (unknown–) began to work as a scriptwriter in the film industry. Her directorial debut did not come until 1995 and was an allegorical story entitled *Accidental Legend*. Set in mainland China it is an unusual mix of adventure, humour and social commentary. After this she directed the children's animation feature *Grandma and Her Ghosts* (1998) which achieved box-office success and has been shown worldwide. In 2004 she directed another children's film entitled *Bear Hug* and in 2010 another film aimed at youth titled *Fantôme, où es-tu?* Wang Siu-di has kept producing television drama, documentaries and commercial shorts in addition to her film works.

Taiwan-born and American-educated Sylvia Chang (1953–) who starred as an actress in more than eighty films, began to direct in 1981. Her directorial works are mostly concerned with women and the various choices that they make in life. She has directed twelve feature films all set in Taipei, Hong Kong and New York and her feature *Siao Yu* (1995) was co-written with Ang Lee. *Tempting Heart* (1999) is a story about first love. *20 30 40* (2004) intertwines the stories of four women: two girls in their twenties dreaming to be singers, a stewardess in her thirties caught between two lovers, and a florist in her forties who discovers that her husband has a second family in the same city. An earthquake that further 'shakes up' everyone's already 'shaky' world comes in the middle of the film and results in the comic connection of the three subplots. Sylvia Chang's latest direction is the comedy-drama *Run Papa Run* (2008) and focuses on a Triad crime boss who attempts to hide his criminal background from his young daughter.

Kyoto-born Kawase Naomi (1969–) won the Camera d'Or at Cannes with her first feature *Suzaku* (1997), becoming the youngest winner of that title. Her second feature *Sharasoju* (2003) received the Grand Jury Prize from Cannes and her 2007 film *The Mourning Forest* won the Grand Prix from Cannes. Her films, certainly those made up unto 2007, reveal the beauty of the Japanese landscape and the understated emotions that exist between people. In 2008, Kawase made *Seven Nights* that follows a young woman's trip to Bangkok and how her encounters with a different culture makes her see herself in new light. In her recent feature *Hanezu* (2011) she again makes a connection between contemporary Japan and its ancient root by adopting imageries from *Manyoshu* (the oldest Japanese poetry classic). In her own words she believes 'there is a deeper truth in the tales of nameless people who are hidden in the shadows of major events and neglected by the trivial riches of the daily media' (Kawase 2011). Kawase Naomi's cinematic style is one that is based on hand-held documentary-style intimate portraits of people and places. She is the first female director from Japan to receive major international recognition and the only woman whose films have recently been screened in Tokyo's small avant-garde theatres.

In the 1990s three notable younger female directors emerged in Japan. Matsuura Masako (1960–) made her first feature film *Secret Liaisons* (1995) ten years after her completion of the film script. With the success of her first film she made a second feature *Deborah is Rival* (1997). Her most acclaimed work to date is *Platonic Sex* (2001) that was adapted from former porn star Iijima Ai's autobiography. The protagonist of the film Ai is gang-raped at the age of seventeen and instead of showing her sympathy her father beats her and throws her out of the house. She begins to work as a 'comfort girl' in bars and then signs a contract with a pornography film company. The film touchingly reveals Ai's encounters in a male-centered society and takes the audience to a world where innocence can easily be traded and destroyed. Unlike many female directors working in the film industry, Mastuura's films, including her most recent feature *Mayu: Star of Heart* (2007), are mostly produced by major film studios such as Toho or Shochiku rather than smaller independent production companies.

Matsunashi Tomoko (1971–) started her film career as an actress for independent films and directed her first two short films *To Be or Not to Be* (1995) and *Cherry Boys Legend* (1996) in 8mm and since then produced a film every one or two years. Matsunashi was, however, not recognised beyond the festival circuit until she made her 2005 feature *The Way of the Director*. Peter Rist calls the film a 'Japanese feminist comedy' (2005) and it is a hilarious and poignant parody of how people exploit each other's bodies, money and creativity in the filmmaking circle and society at large.

In 1996, with the help of female producer Okamoto Mineko, veteran scriptwriter Takayama Yukiko (1945–) finally got a chance to direct and made her award-winning feature *After Wind Has Gone*. Her beautiful and intriguing second feature *Musumedojoji* (a.k.a. *Love of Snake*, 2004) follows a woman's attempt to find out why her twin sister committed suicide by re-living her sister's experiences of love, desire and dance.

The Rise of Women Directors: After 2000

In mainland China a group of female directors who were born in the 1970s came to prominence after 2000. In this group of younger women direc-tors, Li Hong graduated from the Beijing Film Academy directing depart-ment in 1997 (interestingly she was the only women from this cohort ever to actually direct a film). Her first feature *Tutor* (1997) won both domestic and international awards. Her second feature was a made-for-television film shot in 16mm entitled *Black and White* (2003) and tells the tale of a murder in a photography studio. This film led the producers of her next feature to realise her potential in making thrillers and thus her third film, *Curse of Lola* (2005), was advertised as a horror film (even though the director regards it as a thriller about the relationship between one man and each of his three lovers). This film was shown at the Taiwan International Ethnographic Film Festival (TIEFF). In 2011 Li Hong's new film *My Beautiful Boss* was released; it focuses on pervasive brand name images and presents Beijing as an in-ternational metropolitan, but it directly challenges the romantic-comedy genre and popular melodrama by excluding even one kiss scene.

Former TV documentary director Li Yu (1973–) made her first feature film *Fish and Elephant* (2001). She wishes to break what she perceived as the limitations of the documentary form and offer a further exploration on hu-man nature (see Yang and Wei 2009: 247). This wish has been guiding her selection of stories in all her subsequent feature films. *Fish and Elephant* is often regarded as the first lesbian film from mainland China but, together with the more controversial aspects of the story, it also presents a truth-ful reflection of younger women's living conditions in China. A notion of sisterhood is presented as an important and profoundly deep understand-ing between women, and this is combined with documentary-style real-life scenes and footage. Her second feature *Dam Street* (2005) follows a teenage girl's life after her untimely pregnancy. Her third film, *Lost in Beijing* (2007), depicts contemporary Beijing and focuses on two couples' complicated relationship after a rich middle-age massage parlour owner rapes a young female employee. A pregnancy further complicates the situation between the victim, her working-class husband, the rapist and the rapist's wife. Li's films have constantly focused on the everyday decisions that face women in the modern age. The ban of *Lost in Beijing* after its theatrical screening for one month (due to its controversial content) for good or bad boosted Li Yu's fame in China. Her most recent film *Buddha Mountain* (2010), focusing on three energetic and social marginalised Sichuan youth and an elderly opera singer they gradually befriend, once again explores the complex relationship between human beings.

Also working in television before directing, Ma Liwen's *Gone is the One Who Held Me Dearest in This World* (2002) is a project that has come to fruition after a five-year effort. At the age of thirty the director here presents the touching relationship between a mother in her eighties and a daughter in her fifties. *Gone is the One…* really experiments with the on- and off-screen voices of female characters; these voices come in and out of the narrative flow in a way that helps to present a multiplicity of perspectives, making each voice as important as the other by breaking up the normal hierarchy of prioritising the voiceover's credibility. Ma Liwen received wider international attention with her second feature *You and Me* (2005) focusing on the relationship between a young tenant and her landlady in her eighties. She made her first 'commercial' film *Lost and Found* in 2007 and although it achieved only moderate success it served to convince many in the film industry of her ability to make popular and successful films. Her forth feature *Desire of the Heart* (2008) enjoyed larger success with one of the most popular male stars Ge You as the leading actor.

Actress Xu Jinlei (1974–) also directed four films: *Me and My Father* (2001), *Letter from a Strange Woman* (2005), *Dream Into Reality* (2006) and *Go Lala Go!* (2010). While *Me and My Father* depicts a special and convincing story between a father and daughter, *Letter from a Strange Woman* was adapted from Stefan Zweig's novella by the same title and the film raised some controversy in its presentation of women's various attitudes towards love and sex. *Dream Into Reality* challenges the audience's expectations by focusing on a lengthy dialogue between an actress whose acting is not 'coming through' and a director who always misses her points. *Go Lala Go!*, advertised as the Chinese version of *The Devil Wears Prada* (2006), features four actresses and one actor in the latest brand-name fashions and presents Beijing as a flashy and modern city. Xu Jinlei's swing between smaller-budget projects and bigger-budget dramas is obvious in her four directed films to date. She takes advantage of her stardom and status as one of most popular bloggers and makes use of the Internet as a good platform for her on-line magazine and other projects she takes on, thus continuing to raise her profile.

After 2000 four women born in the 1960s and 1970s have established themselves as important independent filmmakers in Hong Kong. Renowned scriptwriter Aubrey Lam has now three feature films to her director's credit. *Twelve Nights* (2000), *Hidden Track* (2003) and *Anna and Anna* (2007) are unusual urban-based stories. Her directing has a distinct style with a luminous dream-like quality that is made 'real' with a variety of trivial details and actions of the protagonists but is imbued with a profound anxiety about future.

Barbara Wong (unknown–) graduated from Hong Kong's Academy of Performing Art before furthering her studies at New York University. Her first notable film was her feature documentary *Women's Private Parts* (2001) which has women from different professions talking frankly about their views on sex and men. Her two later films, *Truth or Dare: 6th Floor Rear Flat* (2003) and *Six Strong Guys* (2004), are both highly ironic urban comedies. Her 2007 feature *Wonder Women*, which was made in commemoration of the ten-year anniversary of Hong Kong's handover, received varied responses from critics and viewers. Her recent work *Breakup Club* (2010) again draws a perfect balance between the parody of, and the concern over, Hong Kong's lost youngsters.

Carol Lai (1966–) studied marketing before turning to filmmaking. Her first feature, *Glass Tear* (2001) tells the story of a relationship between a lonely old man and a runaway girl. Her second feature *Floating Landscape* (2003) focuses on a girl who cannot forget her dead lover and searches for a landscape in one of his paintings. When another man begins to fall in love with her together they begin to recreate the landscape of her dreams. Lai's most recent features are two thrillers: *The Third Eye* (2006) shot in HD and CGI-intensive horror film *Naraka 19* (2007).

Yan Yan Mak (1971–) is an important new directorial voice. Her first feature film *Ge Ge* (2001) screened at the Venice Film Festival and eventually won several awards around the world. Her second feature *Butterfly* (2004) was adapted from the novella *The Mark of the Butterfly* by the Taiwanese writer Can Xue. It tells the touching story of a young woman called Flavia and cuts between her memories of her first love Zhenzhe, the 1989 Tiananmen Square events and her later love affair with the singer Yip (a lesbian relationship which shakes her seemingly happy marriage). Yan Yan Mak's most recent feature *Merry Go Around* (2010) is a modern fable of how a dying girl tries to understand death by working in a place where people store the coffins of their relatives temporarily (for various reasons) and gradually forms a friendship with the 'coffin watcher' who has been waiting for his true love to return.

After directing three hundred 'pink movies' Hamano Sachi finally realised her dream of presenting 'real' women with her first narrative feature, *In Search of a Lost Writer: Wandering in the Seventh World* (2001). The film clearly represents a woman's perspective on the life and work of writer Osaki Midori, a writer whose works are often interpreted very differently by male critics when compared to female ones. What is remarkable is that this film was made with money donated by 12,000 women (see Yang and Wei 2009: 423) and is a remarkable example of female solidarity in making art. Hamano's second narrative feature is *Lily Festival* (2001), a comedy reflecting the issue of sexuality and the elderly, which was loved by audiences from the 28 cities that the film toured to. Her third film *The Cricket Girl* (2005) returns to works by Osaki Midori, who is seen as travelling between the world of her fiction and that of her fictional character's imagination.

There are three more women born in the 1970s who have gained importance in Japan's independent cinema scene after 2000. Ogigami Naoko (1972–) received international attention with her debut film *Barber Yoshino* (2004), a light comedy around a small-town barber house owned by a woman named Yoshino. Ogigami went on to make *Love Is Five Seven Five* (2005), *Kamome Diner* (2006), *Glasses* (2007) and *Toilet* (2010), quickly becoming an important Japanese director on the international film scene. Previously a film student at the University of Southern California, Ogigami's works cross geographical borders as well as boundaries by filming *Kamome Diner* in Canada and *Toilet* in Finland. For her, these locations are not so different from those in Japan as her film world always involves a focus on the unique identity of individual characters. Her films always contain an understated humour and she shows a great awareness of both Japanese culture in relation to other cultures and film language as a tool for expression of emotions.

Hiroshima-born Nishikawa Miwa (1974–) debuted with *Wild Berries* in 2003 and then went on to direct *Female* (2005), *Sway* (2006), *Ten Nights of Dream* (2006) and *Dear Doctor* (2009). Whilst *Sway* broke box-office records in Japanese art-house cinemas, *Dear Doctor* received a major critical success and won the Screenplay of the Year award from the Japanese Academy in 2010. Nishikawa's films explore human nature in depth and show an extremely sensitive touch regarding the vulnerability of characters. Together with Matsunashi and Ogigami she is writing a new chapter in the history of female-made films in Japan and has obtained international recognition alongside other women directors such as Kawase Naomi. What is worthy of mentioning here is that in Japan veteran women scriptwriters, television producers and those in other media fields are beginning to make their first films despite their relatively advanced ages. In 2006, 77-year-old Sembon Yoshiko made her directorial debut with the feature film *Red Whale, White Snake* that focuses on an old man and his granddaughter returning to the home he stayed in during the war.

In Taiwan, the most important women directors to emerge since 2000 are perhaps Zero Chou (1969–) and Lee Yun-chan (1972–). Lee Yun-chan can really be seen as a modern fairytale teller with a camera; from her first short film *Magic Washing Machine* (2004) to her debut feature film *Shoe Fairy* (2006) to her comedy *My DNA Says I Love You* (2007) and the most recent *Dancing with You* (2010), she focuses on the 'reenactment' of fairytale situations. The girl who loves shoes has her feet broken in an accident; the girl who is a fanatical cleaner discovers that her new love does not do his laundry in a timely fashion; and the girl who wants to kill herself gets herself fished out from the bottom of the lake. In true fairytale fashion it then takes love, courage and imagination to set things right again.

The stories of Zero Chou are very different: death, tattoos, same-sex love, drag queens, highways, escape, violence, desperation and flashy costumes all in feature in her films. After making quite a few documentaries, she began to direct feature films from 2004 and now has four features to her director's credit: *Splendid Float* (2004), *The Road on the Air* (2006), *Spider Lilies* (2007) and *Drifting Flowers* (2008).

Other female directors of note include Kuo Chen-ti (1965–) who first achieved critical success for her documentary feature *Chingwen is Not Home* (2000). The success of this helped to secure funding for another documentary feature *Viva Tonal: The Dance Age* (2003). *Viva Tonal* was shot on 16mm and did relatively well on theatrical release. In 2009 she directed her first narrative feature *Step by Step* about how a mysterious dance teacher brings hope to old people living in a care-home. Tseng Wen-chen also began her film career with two award-winning documentaries: *After Championship* (2000) and *Spring: The Story of Hsu Chin-yu* (2002). She has made two narrative feature films to date, the light comedy *Fishing Luck* (2005) and *Amour Legende* (2007); both films focus on searching for the meaning of true love. Cheng Fenfen (1970–) began as a television commercial director and then got into making television drama. She has directed two feature-length films, *Keeping Watch* (2007) and *Hear Me* (2009). With the help of female producer Michelle Yeh, a director even younger than Lee Yun-chan (who was in her early thirties when she first began directing), at the age of twenty-four Chen Yin-yung (1980–) made her debut feature *Formula 17* (2004) a youth-focused drama about the relationship between three homosexual teenage boys. In 2006 she made *Catch* (incidentally with the same crew as that she worked with on *Formula 17*) and in 2009 she took part in *Tawian24H* which features eight stories from different filmmakers chronicling 24 hours in Taipei. Also at the age of twenty-four Hong Kong's Heiward Mak (1984–) directed her first feature *High Noon* (2008), focusing on problem youth in Hong Kong (the film is an update of the Fruit Chan's *Made in Hong Kong* (1997)). Her second feature was an adaption from a self-penned novel entitled *Ex* (2010). When she cannot find the funds to direct, Heiward Mak writes scripts for other local directors.

Yet Another Women's Wave

Focusing on a comparison between Chinese and Japanese cinema along a 'women's trajectory' leads to some paradoxical findings. Among the four regions discussed both mainland China and Hong Kong have a clear trajectory of female directors since the respectively the 1950s and 1930s: in both countries women have been working consistently in the industry. The same cannot be said of women directors in Taiwanese and Japanese cinemas, with women highly marginalised in the film industries of these countries. In the case of Hong Kong I want to argue that the influence of a pioneer woman like Esther Eng was very strong as she became an example of a capable filmmaker within the industry; and the presence of such a pioneer encouraged other women to aspire to be filmmakers. Mainland China once had the largest group of women directors in the world and this situation was clearly helped by the communist system that enforced gender equality in the professional and social lives of women from 1950 to the late 1980s. The literal advantage of large numbers is that it makes 'waves or trends' possible in certain historical periods – as revealed by the two women's film waves taking place in the late 1980s and early 2000s. Proportion-wise however, mainland Chinese women made fewer works revealing feminine consciousness (thus few engaged in serious debates about women and the status of women); and, soon after the reform of the state-owned film industry in 1993, most of them stopped directing films for studios as they failed to make a commercial profit. During the 1980s and 1990s, female directors from Japan and Taiwan, although making fewer films, have revealed a much higher 'feminine consciousness' through their films. This is perhaps due to the fact that they could hardly pass up the fewer opportunities presented to make their voices heard.

Japanese women directors had received nearly no support from the film industry or cultural institutions before the mid-1980s but since then Japanese women have been successfully and energetically producing films in relatively large volume. Like many Chinese female directors, they seem to be most successful in telling stories about love and romance, relationships, family problems, children/youth issues, and in revealing the concerns and experiences of marginalised social groups. Meanwhile, since as a general rule they do not carry and present the gender biases that have been so clichéd in films by male directors (passive women, active men etc), they have gradually received recognition for their creativity that often originates from their own subjective and personal experiences. Each individual woman may feel that she is making films 'independently' but the co-existence of several women all making films is a really important change to the film culture in Japan. A trajectory of women directors is slowly forming in Japanese cinema.

Women directors from Hong Kong have always enjoyed more opportunities than their peers in Taiwan but Taiwanese women have in fact revealed much more of a conscious concern over gender issues in their films. Since Hong Kong women generally enjoyed a higher social status from the 1970s, though the film industry itself has always (and continues to be) very patriarchal, it does not always reject women outright (compared for instance to the Japanese industry). From the 1980s female directors' works on 'women-themed' films have been recognised and sometimes praised and celebrated. In good years like 2002 and 2010 Hong Kong screens have shown four or five good works from female directors within one year bringing delight to its female audience and allowing an increased recognition of the skills and abilities of these women.

Finally as women directors in mainland China persist in their film careers, another wave of women's cinema, with a vibrant blend of commercial and artistic elements, has empowered women's positions as directors in the film industry. Staring with Ma Liwen's *Desire of the Heart*, the wave was followed by Xu Jinglei's *Go Lala Go!*, Li Hong's *My Beautiful Boss* and Yi Meng's *Sophie's Revenge* (2011). In Hong Kong, 'romantic films' have become almost the exclusive specialty of female directors while male directors have been preoccupied with kung-fu sagas and gangster movies. Heiward Mak's *Ex*, Yan Yan Mak's *Merry Go Around* (2010) and Barbara Wong's *Breakup Club* and *Perfect Wedding* (2011) have all breathed fresh air into Hong Kong's theatres. Veteran director Ann Hui has continued directing (though her peers who emerged during the Hong Kong New Wave are in fact rarely making films). Her two recent features *The Way We Are* and *Night and Fog*, set in Tin Shui Wai, one of the poorest areas in Hong Kong's New Territory, have shown continued concern over questions of immigration and female friendship. Her new feature *A Simple Life* portrays an ordinary woman's life in a contemporary setting, keeping to her desire to focus on women's experiences and lives. Veteran scriptwriter Ivy Ho, who wrote for Ann Hui, Peter Chan and others, started directing from 2009 with her debut work *Intimacy* that was followed by *Crossing Hennessy* (2010). Both films won her Hong

Kong critics' script awards. These new waves of women's cinema emerging in Hong Kong and Mainland China are only part of the women's wave in the larger Asian contexts.

Nowadays, in the era of independent production, the advent of digital media and technology and the wide establishment of media schools have allowed young women filmmakers to flower. Mao's statement that 'women can hold up half of the sky' has been cherished by Chinese women for nearly sixty years. Hopefully it will not take too long for women to hold up half of the cinematic sky and they will gain more and more opportunities in China, Japan, Taiwan and elsewhere.

Bibliography

Brennen, Sandra (1998) *Hidari Sachiko*. Online. Available at: http://www.allmovie.com (accessed 4 September 2005).

Du, Yunzhi (1988) *Film History of Republic of China*. Taipei: Cultural Construction Committee.

Huang, Ren (1994) *Taiwanese Language Cinema*. Taipei: Wanxiang.

Johnston, Claire (ed.) (1975) *The Work of Dorothy Arzner: Towards a Feminist Cinema*. London: British Film Institute.

Kaplan, E. Ann (1985) 'Problematizing Cross-cultural Analysis: The Case of Women in the Recent Chinese Cinema', *Wide Angle*, 11.2: 40–50.

Kawase, Naomi (2011) 'Hanezu: A Film by Naomi Kawase' see http://www.festival-cannes.com/assets/Image/Direct/040259.pdf, last retried August 15, 2011.

Kumagai, Hiroko (2004) *Documentary Film Women Make Films: The Tokyo International Women's Film Festival*. Produced by the Tokyo International Women's Film Festival, Tokyo, Japan.

Law, Kar (2001) 'Overview of Hong Kong's New Wave Cinema', in Ether Yau (ed.) *At Full Speed: Hong Kong Cinema in a Borderless World*. Minneapolis: University of Minnesota Press, 31–52.

Law, Kar and Frank Bren (2004) *Hong Kong Cinema: A Cross-Cultural View*. Lanham: Scarecrow Press.

Lei, Qun (1938) 'Female Director Wu Jinxia', in *Singtao Daily*, 15 December.

Lin, Xinghong (2004) unpublished research data.

Lu, Feiyi (1998) *Taiwan Cinema: Politics, Economy, Aesthetics*. Taipei: Yuanliou.

Masumoto, Yumiko (2004) 'Japan', in Yoshida Mayumi, Hayashi Huyuko, Masumoto Yumiko, Takano Etsuko, Otake Yoko and Kotouda Chieko (eds) *Films of the World Women Directors*. Tokyo: Education Material Publisher, 248–68.

McCarthy, Todd (1995) 'Eng's Lost Pix a Chinese Puzzle', in *Variety*, 21–27 August.

Rist, Peter (2005) 'Tomoko Matsunashi: The Way of the Interview.' http://www.offscreen. com/index.php/phile/essays/tomoko_matsunashi/ Last retrieved August 15, 2011.

Wang, Hanlun (1996) 'My Film Career', in Dai Xiaolan (ed.) *Chinese Silent Film*. Beijing: China Film Press, 1473–6.

Wang, Lingzhen (2011) *Chinese Women's Cinema: Transnational Context*. Columbia: Columbia University Press.

Xue, Huiling and Wu Junhui (1994) *The Era of Taiwanese Language Cinema*. Taipei: National Film Archive.

Yang, Yuanying (1996) *Her Voices: Recounts from Ten Chinese Female Directors*. Beijing: Social Science Press.

Yang, Yuanying and S. Louisa Wei (2009) *Women's Cinema: Dialogues with Chinese and Japanese Female Directors*. Shanghai: Eastern China Normal University Press.

Yau, Ching (2004) *Filming Margins: Tang Shu Shuen, a Forgotten Hong Kong Woman Director*. Hong Kong: Hong Kong University Press.

Ye, Longyan (1996) *Xinzhu Film History 1900–1995*. Taipei: Xinzhu Municipal Cultural Centre.

Yoshida, Mayumi (2001) *Films of World Women Filmmakers*. Tokyo: Kyoiku Shiryoo Shuupansha.

Yu, Muyun (1997) *History of Hong Kong Cinema, Volume II: The 1930s*. Hong Kong: Sub-cultural Books.

Fusion Cinema: The Relationship Between Jia Zhangke's Films *Dong* and *Still Life*

Barbara Jenni

The two films I am going to primarily discuss here were both directed in 2005, when the Chinese director Jia Zhangke followed his good friend and painter Liu Xiaodong to Fengjie in the Three Gorges Region in Southwest China. Liu had been there before and had done some paintings of this region and its people that would disappear with the Three Gorges Dam that spans the Yangtze River and that became fully operational in 2011 (after these films were completed). Liu returned to Fengjie to do another painting series focusing on the demolition workers, and asked Jia to come with him to make a documentary on his work. When on location, Jia decided to make a fictional film as well, so the final results of this journey were two films: *Still Life* (*Sanxia haoren*, literally 'Decent People of the Three Gorges'), winner of the Golden Lion for Best Film at the 63rd Venice Film Festival in 2006, and *Dong* (meaning 'East'), a documentary on the work of Liu Xiaodong.

This article mainly deals with the 'provocative relationship', as Shelly Kraicer puts it, between the two films (2006). It develops from the fact that both films share some material, i.e. they share some literal film sequences and scenes, despite the fact that *Dong* is labelled a documentary movie, whereas *Still Life* is a fictional film. One of the questions that is therefore raised is related to the concept of reality that Jia uses in his work as well as several other elements that are worth noting and considering. I suggest that *Dong* is a 'hybrid documentary' because it contains some scenes that are not simply taken out of a fictional movie by the same director, but belong in both movies and thus are an indicator of Jia's overstepping the borders of the traditional film genres. I would even go one step further and call Jia's cinema 'fusion cinema', by which I mean Jia's blurring of the genres, the combination of personal and artistic life which Jia does when he invites his friends and family to take over parts in his movies, in hiring nonprofessional actors, and the fact that both Jia's films and Liu's paintings are important works regarding the ongoing controversy in several artistic fields over the Three Gorges Dam on the Yangste River (for which more than a million people had to be relocated) and whole cities like Fengjie had to be displaced to higher altitudes. The fusion is an extending of the hybridisation as it involves more than filmic genres.

Intrinsic facts within the two films, concerns in others of Jia's films, and the relationship between Jia and Liu and their respective work are of great importance. The titles of the movies, the shared scenes, particularly a scene that begins in one of the films and continues in the other will be analysed in detail. Also, the figure of Han Sanming, one of the main characters in *Still Life*, who is highly important especially in the context of other films by Jia. Last but not least, not only the personal relationship between Jia and Liu is considered here, but also the links between their works and painting and filming in general. With reference to all the above, *Dong* is a two-section film with three main elements regarding the content: in the first part, Jia and his camera follow Liu Xiaodong on his journey to the Three Gorges Region where he is working on a series of paintings of demolition workers which he eventually titles 'Hot Bed'. He is shown directing the scenes he wants to paint, taking photographs of them, sketching and painting in oil. This is interrupted by short interview sequences. Among the workers Liu is painting is Sanming, the main protagonist of *Still Life*, and he features in several more scenes that the two movies share. When one of the workers he uses as a model dies accidentally, Liu drives to his family to get to know them and to give them some photographs of the deceased and gifts for his children.

The second part of the film takes place in Thailand, where Liu paints a series of women that he arranges on beds and sofas and surrounds with fruits. When there is a flood one of the models returns to her hometown to look for her family, but this time, the camera does not go with her. There are some interview scenes with Liu Xiaodong in the second part as well. The main aspects of this documentary are therefore the place where he is working, Liu's ideas and conceptions about his work, and his connections with people.

Why was the title *Dong* chosen for this documentary? The Three Gorges Region lies in the Southwest of China, and Thailand is Southwest of China, so, at first glance, both regions do not have anything to do with 'the East'. There are two aspects the title hints at: one is Liu Xiaodong's given name, the other is the European perception of both China and Thailand as part of the East.

The literal meaning of Liu's first name, Xiaodong, is 'little East'. Liu was born in 1963, and it was common at that time to name a child with characters praising the communist regime of China and China as the Eastern part of the world (as in *Dongfang hong, The East is Red*, which was the de facto anthem of China promoting Maoism during the 1960s). As *Dong* is a documentary on Liu's work, to name it after the person who is being portrayed seems a logical step.

The second association could be called provocative. Both China and Thailand are in the Eastern part of the world from a European, or, let us say, Western, perspective. From a Eurocentric point of view, Liu shows us the 'East' as we imagine it and even reinforces some clichés about it: in the Western Media China is seen as a country of economic boom, the destruction of nature, super fast construction and demolition, and hundreds of accidents (mining etc) in which a lot of innocent people die; whereas Thailand is still seen as (in)famous for sex tourism and beautiful women. When he chooses to paint men of the lowest social class in China and young women arranged among exotic fruits in Thailand, these clichés are subjects that might come to the mind of a European viewer watching his works. The film includes one scene where a Thai prostitute is watched by the camera approaching men in a street, and another in which two blind men walk singing through a market in order to earn money. Via these scenes the real reason that a lot of Western people go to Thailand for their holidays is suggested as there are many Westerners crossing the path of the two singers.

Dong is labelled a documentary movie but the fact that some scenes that appear in a fictional movie also appear in a non-fictional one (and being announced as fiction) raises the question of 'labelling'. In order to examine this question of filmic 'labelling', we first have to agree on a definition regarding documentary films, and list some typical characteristics of that genre. This is not an easy thing to do, as the considerable amount of literature on that topic demonstrates! In a nutshell, the common understanding among filmmakers and film critics, and probably most viewers, is that the expectation towards a documentary is different than towards a fictional film. In a documentary, we expect a 'fair and honest representation of somebody's experience of reality' (Aufderheide 2007: 3), while in a fictional movie, the freedom of expression of the director is much broader and the viewer accepts more manipulation through lighting, staging, framing, sound and so on.

It is the 'fair and honest representation' that is queried in *Dong*. When Jia uses scenes in both movies without making this explicit to the viewer, one might think that this is not exactly what one would call 'fair and honest'. But, again, this is not disrespectful in any way, just an extremely subjective conception of reality and filmmaking. Jia is loyal to some respective characteristics of the documentary genre in all his movies, and in *Dong* he mixes the genres and blurs the boundaries in a very uncommon, provocative way. As mentioned, the product of this mingling could be called 'hybrid', in the same sense in that this word has been used in the term 'hybrid genre' since the 1980s. The term is used especially in literature theory, but also in social theory, and refers to types of texts, movies and other cultural products that unite features of different genres.

Shelly Kraicer described the connection between *Dong* and *Still Life* as follows:

As Jia maps it, cinema does not divide neatly into fiction and documentary. *Dong* creates a subjective world, as much inside the mind of the artist Liu as outside in objective space. *Still Life* digs deep to reveal an underlying reality, mobilising sophisticated formal strategies to create images of truth. These same strategies demand – or, rather, construct, during the process of watching – viewers who are ready to watch, absorb, and feel this vision. (2006)

It is not just *Dong* and *Still Life* but all of Jia's works – including his more recent documentaries *Useless* (2009) and *I Wish I Knew* (2010) – which share the same approach to reality: it is always a construction of every individual. Moreover, they share the realistic attitude of showing nonprofessional actors, the extensive use of natural lighting, scenes shot on location and so on, that give the viewer the impression of a 'naturalistic' film, a film created with the same technique most documentaries are. Jia himself stated that in his opinion, 'absolute objectivity' is impossible; there is only 'the director's attitude, how he sees the world and the cinema' (in Teo 2001) and at the time of filming *Dong* he was one of the very few directors of the Sixth Generation who worked in this genre.

Chris Berry analysed a tendency among the Sixth Generation filmmakers that he calls 'getting real'. For him, this term has two implications. First, 'it indicates the drive to represent the "real"' and second, 'it also refers to the slang phrase "get real", meaning "wise up" or "stop dreaming"' (2007: 115). Both these directions are obviously found in Jia's work when he depicts normal people with their ordinary lives and tells us realistic stories that, in most cases, do not have happy endings, but just the endings one might expect for one's own life. It is not dreaming that Jia wants his viewer and his protagonists to do; he wants them to be part of, and therefore view, ordinary lives. Thus, he chooses to show us reality as he or the characters in his films perceive it which cannot be anything but subjective as in Jia's conception everyone sees the world with his or her own eyes. This approach towards reality is the basis for all his films, and which becomes even more apparent in *Dong*, in which he advances the concept of fusion cinema further than before.

The main subject of Berry's essay referenced above is the Chinese documentary that has been innovative and blooming since 1989, and he mentions that the same term, 'on-the-spot-realism', has been used for new documentary as well as for 'the contemporary urban films made by the younger generation of feature filmmakers' (2007: 122). The term seems to suit Jia's work very well, as he admits that a lot of scenes in his movies are created only on location, and have never been written (see Mas n.d.). Furthermore, Jia does both documentary and fiction, and mixes these genres within *Dong*. For *Still Life*, one may use the term 'on-the-spot' in one more sense, as the idea to make this movie only occurred to Jia when he was in Fengjie with Liu Xiaodong.

Still Life focuses on two main narratives: Han Sanming, a coal miner, is coming to the Three Gorges Region to look for his wife and daughter. Sixteen years earlier he had brought his wife to Shanxi Province but subsequently both his wife and daughter were removed by the police. His wife's new job on the ferry means that Sanming has to wait in Fengjie a couple of months for her return, so in the meantime, he starts working as a demolition worker and lives in a small and cheap boarding house. When he finally meets his wife, she decides to go back with him, but he has to promise to take over a family debt. If he is able to raise 30,000 RMB within a year, she will be allowed to go to Shanxi. Sanming cannot see their daughter as she, according to her mother, has gone 'somewhere South' for work.

The main female character, Shen Hong, originating from Shanxi Province as well, is coming to the area in search for her husband, Guo Bin, whom she has not seen in over two years. Guo Bin is working for the demolition authority and probably involved in some illegal business dealings. First, the viewer gets the impression that Shen Hong wants her husband back as she reacts jealously about rumours regarding another woman, but when the two of them finally meet through the help of a common friend Shen Hong asks Guo Bin for a divorce in order to be able to marry her new boyfriend.

The two stories are connected by the figure of Brother Mark, a young employee of Guo Bin who meets Sanming by accident. The two men become friends but then Brother Mark dies in a brawl.

Some side lines of the two narratives deal with figures who will have to move places due to the flooding of the city (which took place in 2003) and some of these marginal characters decide to go as far as Guangdong on the southern coast to try out a new life. The fate of Sanming's daughter represents a well-known pattern in China: young, badly educated people have to leave their families to work for low wages in factories somewhere in China, and a lot of them see their families only once a year, during the Chinese New Year Break.

The ambiance of the film is, despite a lot of humorous scenes, a melancholic one. Jia has an empathetic way of telling stories about normal people struggling through their lives and of showing their endurance and their ability to suffer. By choosing the consequences of the Three Gorges Dam as the subject of his movie, he shows his interest in ongoing social processes of great importance in contemporary Chinese society and arguably the world, and as in all of his movies up to today, he focuses on normal people, the so called *laobaixing* ('those who bear one of the hundred surnames'), for whom the construction project is daily reality.

As already noted, in Chinese the film is entitled *Sanxia haoren*, which literally can be translated as 'Decent People of the Three Gorges'. Why was *Still Life* chosen as the international title? One of the reasons must be the length and rather unpoetic nature of the literal translation, but there is more to it than that. The term *Still Life* not only arouses associations with painting, but also of the cinematic or photographic still that is a momentary record of a scene, just as 'Still Life' is in painting. In European painting history, 'Still Life' was established as a genre during the seventeenth century and has been especially popular in the Netherlands. The term 'Still Life' is usually applied to representation of objects, such as flowers, food, tableware and so on. Lighting, colouring and arrangement are of even greater importance in a 'Still Life' than in any other genre of painting, and in that lies a parallel to film in which all these aspects are of great importance as they make up a large part of what produces the 'illusion' in film. In documentary movies, too, though to a lesser extent than in fictional films, lighting, sound and arrangement can have a highly manipulating effect on the viewer. In traditional Chinese painting, 'Still Life' as a genre has never existed, but nonetheless, some elements of the concepts were shared in Landscape or Bird and Flower Painting. I will return to these points later, when considering the relationship between Jia and Liu as well as film and painting.

The literal meaning of *Still Life* might also be part of the meaning of the film, as 'life' stands still in Fengjie during these days. Although people are working and moving and a lot of things are happening, this specific life will end in a certain way at the moment of the flooding.

The Chinese title with the literal meaning of 'Decent People of the Three Gorges' refers much more to what is Jia's main topic in all of his films: normal people, the *laobaixing*. These people include the owner of the boarding house to whom Sanming tries to talk but is having difficulties to make himself understood, as they use different dialects. They also include the workers Sanming shares his room with at the boarding house and who show him their home scenery on a bill, and so on.

As mentioned, *Still Life* and *Dong* share three scenes: (1) when Sanming passes a house that is knocked down, a wall is collapsing; (2) some demolition workers (including Sanming) are shown hammering bricks and some liquid is sprayed onto walls and bricks; (3) Sanming is standing in front of a banister and watching the scenery.

The fourth scene I will describe here is one that offers a narrative continuation if not literally filmic scenes. In *Dong*, there are some men carrying a corpse covered by a blanket on a wooden panel away from the place of demolition; Sanming is walking behind them. This scene seems to continue in *Still Life*, when the same transport of the corpse is shown towards the river and finally putting the panel and four men with it on a boat while Sanming is left on the bank.

Scene 1: Collapsing Wall

In this short scene, Sanming is passing a house and while he walks away from it, we see one of the walls collapsing.

In *Still Life*, this scene is shown at the beginning of the movie, when Sanming goes to the pier in search for his wife's brother. In *Dong*, this scene takes place before the death of one of the demolition workers.

The meaning of this scene is the same in both films: it is intended to give the viewer some impression of how this demolition work proceeds, and how the house collapses – in order to show that this is the normal course of things in Fengjie before the flooding. There are no bystanders watching the scene which demonstrates all the more that such events are commonplace in those days.

Scene 2: Sprayers and Demolition Workers

This scene shows topless workers hammering and breaking bricks in the same rhythm and several men in protective overalls including face masks going through empty rooms spraying some kind of liquid on the floor. The order of the two sequences is changed in the movies: while in *Dong*, the sprayers are shown before the workers tearing down a house, in *Still Life* the workers come first. This scene with the workers seems not to be staged, but recorded on the spot. One hint is that the workers are wearing helmets, while in other scenes that seem more staged they are more often than not working without helmets. In contrast, the scene with the sprayers seems to be staged as it is not totally clear or understandable what they are doing: if their goal is to protect the demolition workers from poisonous dust or any other kind of danger coming from the tearing down of old building material their work appears not thorough enough as they spray rather cursorily. One could also imagine that they want to destroy any insects or germs that might be left over from former occupants but in this case they work too superficially to have any effect. The workers' part of the scene seems to be inserted to show the poetic beauty demolition work can have when all the workers with their half-naked bodies work in the same rhythm and do the same movements; it has the flavour of a dance scene. The sprayer sequence gives the director an opportunity to hint at relics of former residents as there are still certificates and posters hanging on the walls. For the viewer, this might raise the question as to where these people may have gone and why they left certain things behind, and furthers the sense of loss they certainly must have experienced in their forced relocation from the area.

Scene 3: Sanming Watching the Scenery
In this scene, Sanming is just standing in his underwear before a balustrade and watching the scenery below him. In *Dong* Sanming is painted in the scenes coming before and after that, but in *Still Life* the scene is not directly connected yet stands on its own. This results in different meanings in *Still Life* and *Dong*.

In *Dong* this scene has a totally different context: Sanming is one of the models that are painted by Liu Xiaodong. They have to sit or stand still for him for quite a long time so Sanming might be enjoying the scenery during a break and relaxing and stretching his legs and knees as he is painted crouching. In *Dong* it is clear that the whole painting process takes place on the platform limited by the balustrade shown, and the scene suits the context naturally.

These three shared scenes show how much information a single scene can contain in a film and of how much importance it can be. They also show how much manipulating takes place in a movie, and they make *Dong* into a 'hybrid' documentary, which is a term I will explain in more detail below. As we have seen, manipulation is accepted to a different extent in documentaries and fictional features, which will be a point in my analysis later on.

The Continued Scene: Corpse Transport

This scene is of great importance as it does not really consist of shared material but is an array of scenes that begins in *Dong* and continues in *Still Life*. In both films we see a wooden shelf with a flowery blanket on top of it and the context indicates that there is a corpse lying in between. Through the context of the two movies this signifier stands for two signifieds: in *Still Life*, it is Brother Mark who was found dead under a pile of stones in one of the demolition locations. The day before he had participated in a brawl and not returned within the agreed time. We know this because we have seen Sanming waiting for him in a restaurant. So Sanming tries his cell phone and then finds the corpse by locating the ringing phone. Afterwards, he is shown in front of a picture of Brother Mark on the pile he lies buried under, lighting cigarettes for him and paying his last respects. Then follows the mentioned scene. In *Dong*, shelf and blanket stand for an anonymous demolition worker and tell us the reason for Liu's journey to the hometown of the deceased man.

As mentioned before, the two scenes in the two films form a sequence: the first part happens in *Dong* when the corpse is carried away from the demolition site by four men and Sanming is walking behind them. Then the sequence continues in *Still Life* as the same shelf and blanket with the same figures are shown near a river and boarding a boat. Only Sanming is left behind on the shore. Were the two scenes not spread across two films they would make a perfect sequence with just a single cut in between.

This symbolic representation of death bears some provocation: it stands for a dead man and for a dead figure in a film. I do not want to imply that Jia is not treating the anonymous dead worker with respect; the fact that he included this part in *Dong* speaks against that. Still, if he as director decides to take a blanket and a shelf and let it stand for a dead *man* in one film and a dead *figure* in another then this is a remarkable act, uncommented upon by the director. The fact that the continued sequence deals with the delicate subject of death does not make it easier to handle this provocation. (This provocative relationship between content, form and meaning is something that Jia has explored in several of his later documentaries including *Useless*, *I Wish I Knew* and *24 City* (2009).)

Of course, the viewer only realises these things after having seen both films. But once having noticed it, there are several questions raised by that very fact: what are the consequences of Jia's mixing up documentary and fictional film material? Can we learn anything about his concept of reality from it?

In an interview with Stephen Teo, when asked about the numerous long takes in his movies (*Platform* (2000) in this case), Jia said: 'If I were to cut the scene into pieces, there would be a lot more subjective things that I put in' (in Teo 2001). We can adapt this reply with regard to any scene in Jia's films and come to an understanding of the basic conception of Jia's filmmaking. Every cut is a subjective decision and adds a subjective view point to the things presented in it. For Jia the scene with the death transport in both *Still Life* and *Dong* is a depiction of death, without any disparaging treatment of the deceased man in real life. We never see the person who died, not even on the photographs Liu gives to his family. But we see the family's mourning and remembering of the deceased. The use of the same sign with shared signifier but not signified in two films of a different genre can thus be interpreted as a case of an extremely subjective creation: Jia not only created the sign, he also provided it with the ambiguity of referring to two different men by putting it into both movies. In ordinary conversations, including documentary films as they aspire to show an authentic reality, the goal normally is to make the used signs unambiguous so that misunderstandings can be avoided. Jia's subjective decision to include shelf and blanket in *Dong* only creates its ambiguity, and transfers the duty of reading the sign and choosing between its different meanings to the viewer. This interpretation process is subjective as well. From this analysis of the symbolic representation of death in *Dong* and *Still Life*, we can also conclude that Jia Zhangke expects his audience to be not just viewers but interpreters as well.

The fusion, the sharing of scenes, not only is important for *Dong*, though that is my main point of departure; prior knowledge of *Dong* also changes the interpretation of *Still Life*.

The Triple Identity of Han Sanming

The protagonist Han Sanming in the two movies is a similar case as the sign of shelf and blanket referencing to a deceased in that it shares the signifier but not the signified in different movies.

Han Sanming is a cousin of Jia Zhangke and has played in two of Jia's films before *Still Life* (*Platform* and *The World* (2004)). In *Still Life*, he plays 'Han Sanming', a coal miner from Shanxi Province coming to Fengjie in the Three Gorges Region. That protagonists in films bear the same name their actors are called in reality is a very common thing in Jia's films. What strikes me as important in *Still Life* is that only Sanming has the same name, whereas the protagonist that actress Zhao Tao is playing is called Shen Hong.

Han Sanming acts in a double sense: the nonprofessional actor Han plays the role of Han Sanming, the coal miner, which is temporarily 'playing the role of', i.e. working as, a demolition worker. This complexity grows even more when in *Dong*, Han Sanming is shown as one among the demolition workers that are painted by Liu Xiaodong. Whereas those earn their money as demolition workers in 'real life', Han Sanming is painted as one of them, though in fact, he is not. So, in *Dong*, Han Sanming has a triple identity: he is Han Sanming the actor, Han Sanming the protagonist, and Han Sanming the protagonist-as-model who is painted by Liu Xiaodong. It is in the third identity that he is walking behind that corpse of a 'fellow-worker' when it is carried away from the house in demolition where he assumedly found his death. And it is the protagonist Han Sanming who walks past a house of which one wall is collapsing.

This triple identity emerges through the fact that Han Sanming bears the same name in film and in real life, through the shared scenes, and through his body on which the three identities are united in one.

Han Sanming has played a similar role in *The World*. He appears as the relative of a construction worker that has come to death at work. Sanming (the name of the figure) comes to Beijing to collect the body, and compensation from the construction company. In *Platform*, Han Sanming is also cast as the eponymous figure, this time a coal miner near Fenyang in Shanxi province. It is probably there that Jia discovered the 'real-life miner' as actor.

For the painter, the point of departure is different: as Liu Xiaodong is especially interested in the bodies of his models in the 'Hot Bed' series Han Sanming suits the picture just fine for him, as he in fact has the body of one of these demolition workers who probably have been doing other jobs in their lives as well, be it as farmers or boatmen. For the painter, therefore, Han's identity is of no importance, it is just his body he is interested in. This is also why, as he found Han Sanming in the Three Gorges Region, he paints him there although he must have been aware of Han's standing as an actor for Jia. So, similar to Jia's movies in which three different identities are united on Han Sanming's body, in Liu's paintings, communication is established through the body, not via names or narratives. Liu's anonymous figures mainly are a representation of a social phenomenon, while their individual personality and destiny is not subject of his paintings.

There are other actors that are Jia 'regulars': Zhao Tao, playing Shen Hong in *Still Life*, appears in *24 City*, *Platform* and *The World* (in *The World* she appears under her own name of Tao). The use of the same actors in several films makes the complete works by Jia Zhangke a fusion, and the much used term of a 'universe created by a certain director' can easily be applied here: the recurrent faces as well as the sameness of the names give the regular Jia-viewer the impression of watching the characters develop and progress further in their lives, in one single life instead of several ones in every film.

The shared scenes in the case of *Dong* and *Still Life* take this impression even further when they may convey in the viewer seeing two aspects of one story in the each film. This is in fact not true and this provocative relationship between the films can be seen as a trademark feature of Jia's work.

Personal and professional relationships

As Jia Zhangke stated in several interviews, he was a good friend of Liu Xiaodong's for a long time. Because of this personal relationship Liu has played a small role in Jia's *The World*. A genuine interest in filmmaking on the part of Liu shows in the fact that he has been involved in the production of several films by directors of the so-called Sixth or Urban Generation, which Jia forms part of (as do Wang Xiaoshuai, Zhang Yuan and Lou Ye, to name the most prominent filmmakers).

With regard to their aesthetic relationship, Jia and Liu share a stylistic mode of expression that is roughly called 'realism', but is divided into several undercurrents in Chinese film and painting: both of them are interested in showing human bodies and human relationships as they are perceived by a subjective viewer. The postmodern approach towards reality, similar to the conception of history that the New Historicists apply, seems to suit both of them: reality as well as history are not phenomena that can be understood objectively, as every individual, being part of reality and history, has a certain angle of perception and reality is subjective to everyone. So, what both Jia in his films – be they documentaries or fictional movies – as well as Liu in his paintings depict is their subjective interpretation of reality.

In the case of Jia, Jason McGrath has put forward the thesis that his 'urban realism' draws upon two sources:

> The first source is the broader indigenous movement of postsocialist realism that arose in both documentary and fiction filmmaking in China in the early 1990s ... Nevertheless, the realism of his films must also be understood in the context of a second source, namely the tradition of international art cinema – in particular a type of aestheticised long-take realism that became prominent in the global film festival and art house circuit by the late 1990s (2007: 82)

The postsocialist realism can be broadened to the field of painting, as the so-called 'New Generation' of painters, such as Liu Xiaodong, having graduated from the academies in the late 1980s or early 1990s (around the same time as the Sixth Generation exponents graduated from the Film Academy), share the same approach and interest with filmmakers. Early works of Liu's are counted as works of 'Cynical Realism', whereas the 'Hot Bed' series with their shifted focus on ordinary people, migrant workers and so on, could be called just realistic, and are close to the New Documentary Movement Chris Berry has considered (see also Ou 2006).

When asked in a joint interview about their impressions of the journey to the Three Gorges Region both Jia and Liu said that the collaboration was very natural, and that they especially shared a common way of approaching people and dealing with the question how to portray them and their conditions of life. They both agreed that normal people have a certain kind of innate beauty (see Deng and Wang 2006: 74). This statement affirms their proximity both stylistically and in a broader aesthetic conception of the world.

There are other cultural workers appearing in Jia's movies: Xi Chuan, a poet and professor at the Central Academy of Fine Arts in Beijing, plays the role of the teacher of a culture troupe in *Platform*, and Wang Xiaohui, fellow-director of Jia's, appears next to Liu Xiaodong as a rich man in *The World*. All these men are members of the same generation that was born in the early 1960s and share their process of maturation and growth during the hard times of the Cultural Revolution. When Jia integrates his personal friends into his films, he performs another kind or fusion pointing at a similar aspect as the recurrent actors: he creates a universe in his work and mingles real life with life in films.

Over the last decade Jia has become one of the most well established filmmakers working today. Since his first feature film *Xiao Wu* (1997) and in his subsequent features including *Platform*, *Dong*, *Still Life*, *24 City* and *Useless*, he has demonstrated a critical understanding (and critiquing) of the globalised world in which we all reside. *Useless* is a meditative triptych on the meaning of clothing in modern China. This documentary examines the various stages that clothing goes though from literal creation in large Chinese factories to the creative work of Chinese fashion designer Ma Ke and the hectic Paris Fashion week. *24 City* examines the lives of three generations of family in Chengdu as modernisation takes hold. Like *Dong* and *Still Life*, *24 City* is a hybrid of fictional and documentary elements. *I Wish I Knew* is an examination of the history of Shanghai told by a series of non-chronological narratives. Featuring Jia regular Zhao Tao, the film once again blends notions of documentary and fiction in an examination of modern China. As the Chinese cultural philosopher Wang Min'an asserts (in a discussion with the author in Beijing on 13 March 2005), Jia is one of the few figures on the Chinese cultural scene possessing serious artistic force and an ability to challenge and confront contemporary issues and problems. This essay has utilised the terms 'provocative' and 'hybrid' to describe Jia's work and the films he has produced, since *Dong* consistently supports Howard Feinstein's statement that Jia is 'that rare breed of filmmaker capable of combining stunning artifice with documentary truth' (2009). Films such as *Dong* and *Still Life* demonstrate the new and extremely subjective filmmaking style that Jia has pioneered throughout his career.

Bibliography

Aufderheide, Patricia (2007) *Documentary Film: A Very Short Introduction*. New York: Oxford University Press.

Berry, Chris (2007) 'Getting Real: Chinese Documentary, Chinese Postsocialism', in Zhang, Zhen (ed.) *The Urban Generation: The Urban Generation. Chinese Cinema and Society at the Turn of the Twenty-First Century*. Durham and London: Duke University Press, 115–36.

Deng, Xin and Nan Wang (2006) 'Exchange between Film and Painting. An Interview with Liu Xiaodong and Jia Zhangke', *Eastern* Art, 1, 66–79.

Feinstein, Howard (2009) Films of the Decade: *Still Life*. Online available at <http://www.salon.com/entertainment/movies/film_salon/2009/12/23/Feinstein>(accessed 13th August 2011).

Kraicer, Shelly (2006) 'Chinese Wasteland: Jia Zhangke's, *Still Life*', *Cinemascope*, 29. Online. Available at: http://www.cinema-scope.com/cs29/feat_kraicer_still.html (accessed 14 January 2008).

Mas, Stéphane (n.d.) *Jia Zhang Ke - Interview*. Online. Available at: http://peauneuve.net/article.php3?id_article=171 (accessed 14 January 2008).

McGrath, Jason (2007) 'The Independent Cinema of Jia Zhangke: From Postsocialist Realism to a Transnational Aesthetic', in Zhen Zhang (ed.) *The Urban Generation: The Urban Generation. Chinese Cinema and Society at the Turn of the Twenty-First Century*. Durham and London: Duke University Press, 81–114.

Ou, Ning (n.d.) *Liu Xiaodong and the Sixth Generation Films*. Online. Available at: http://www.alternativearchive.com/en/news/20060301-3.htm (accessed 14 January 2008).

Tao, Stephen (2001) *Cinema with An Accent – Interview with Jia Zhangke, director of Platform*. Online. Available at: http://www.sensesofcinema.com/contents/01/15/zhangke_interview.html (accessed 14 January 2008).

Filmography

Xiao Wu, 1997. Dir. Jia Zhangke. China: Hu Tong Communication.

Platform (Zhantai), 2000. Dir. Jia Zhangke. China: Artcam International.

The World (Shijie), 2004. Dir. Jia Zhangke. China/Japan: Office Kitano.

Dong, 2006. Dir. Jia Zhangke. China: Xstream Pictures.

Still Life (Sanxia haoren), 2006. Dir. Jia Zhangke. China: Shanghai Film Studio.

Useless (*Wú yòng*), 2007. Dir Jia Zhangke. China/Japan: China Film Association and the Mixmind Art and Design Company.

24 City (*Èr shí sì chéng jì*), 2008. Dir. Jia Zhangke. China: Bandia Visual Company, Office Kitano, Shanghai Film Group, XStream Pictures.

I Wish I Knew (*Hai shang chuan qi*), 2010. Dir Jia Zhangke. China: Bojie Media, NCU Group, Shanghai Film Group Corporation, Xingyi Shijie, Xstream Films, Yiming International Media Productions.

From the Art House to the Mainstream: Artistry and Commercialism in Zhang Yimou's Filmmaking

Xin Wang

Unquestionably China's best-known and most controversial filmmaker, Zhang Yimou largely introduced China's cinema to the world. He is one of the most acclaimed members of the well-known 'fifth-generation' filmmakers in China, a cohort who studied at Beijing Film Academy from 1978 to 1982.[1] Zhang is not only famous for his 'art' films in the later 1980s and early 1990s but also for his martial art films since 2004 as well as his artistic involvement in the Beijing Olympics in 2008. His films are known for their transnational audiences and have been well represented at various international film festivals (see Lu 2001) and his work has received considerable academic engagement. This article examines the three stages and genres of his films with the aim of exploring how his filmmaking has evolved from artistic presentations with strong cultural and social criticism to market-oriented entertainment productions, and how his films delicately reflect different stages of the social, cultural and economic changes in China since 1978.

---

1   The term 'fifth-generation filmmakers' was used to distinguish themselves from the previous generations of Beijing Film Academy graduates from 1905–32, 1932–49, 1950–60 and 1960–80.

'Yellow Earth' as Cultural *Habitus*

Whilst Zhang was studying at the Film Academy, the nation was undertaking economic reforms and serious discussions on Chinese cultural identity. Intellectuals, artists and writers returned to public life and engaged in a nationwide debate about the nature and essence of Chinese civilisation and its differences from Western civilisation. Many writers questioned what it meant to be Chinese in the modern world and such a 'values crisis' stimulated Chinese writers to search for their cultural roots. Han Shaogong's article *Wenxue de gen* ('the roots of literature') in 1984 introduced the term *xungen wenxue* ('literary works which are searching for cultural roots') (1986: 1). 'Root-seeking' writers, such as Mo Yan and Yu Hua, often present conflicting values between tradition/modernisation and humanity/nature in their works. These literary works provided rich resources for young filmmakers and inspired them to join the national discourse on the 'cultural roots' through their filmmaking.

Zhang's early films explore these issues of culture and modernity in creative and complex ways. He was born and raised in Xi'an, an ancient capital of China located in the heart of the Yellow Earth Plateau, also known as the Loess Plateau. Symbolically, both the Yellow River and the Yellow Earth Plateau have been regarded as the cradle of Chinese civilisation, characterised as earth-bound, land-attached, agriculture-based and relationship-oriented (see Huang 1997; Yutang 1998). During the 'seeking for cultural roots' movements, the Yellow River and the Yellow Earth Plateau were characterised as a metaphor to symbolise the static, agrarian and inward-looking culture of Chinese civilisation. Fifth-generation filmmakers revealed the 'Yellow Earth' habitus, culture and sentiment in films such as *Yellow Earth* (Chen Kaige, 1984) and *Old Well* (Wu Tianming, 1986). *Yellow Earth* tells a story of an army soldier who goes to a remote village in search of folk songs. Zhang Yimou served as a cinematographer for this film and he also played a leading role in *Old Well*, which tells the story of two neighbouring villages on the Yellow Earth Plateau fighting for water sources. The film was directed by Wu Tianming, the chief of the Xi'an Film Studio and patron of Zhang, and reveals a long-held tradition of this land-based civilisation – to live and die at the same place left by ancestors rather than explore the outside world.

Both films presented and constructed the *habitus* (see Boudieu 1990: 52–65) where the deep-rooted Chinese tradition and culture is located.

The question at the centre of intellectual discussions of the 1980s and 1990s was whether the 'Yellow Earth' culture would still fit the economic modernisation taking place inside China. Contrasted to the far-reaching, expeditionary maritime culture of 'Blue Ocean' Western civilisation, this land-based civilisation was criticised by many scholars and intellectuals as a barrier to democratisation, modernisation and Westernisation.[2] The Chinese intellectual tradition of *youhuan* ('ethos of crisis') and cultural self-criticism helped Zhang form his discourse on Chinese culture and the motif of his early 'root-seeking' films. As someone with an intimate relationship with this *habitus*, he wanted to use his films to express his understanding about the cultural milieu and the psyche of the inhabitants of this land.

First Stage: Films as Discourse on Culture

Zhang's first feature movie, *Red Sorghum*, was produced in 1988 at Xi'an Film Studio. The screen script is based on the first two chapters of the novel by Mo Yan. Zhang adopts the narrative style to tell a story about a village couple, 'my grandma' and 'my grandpa', and their unusual romance and fights against bandits and Japanese invaders. The film uses bright red and yellow to reveal the deep-rooted cultural and social tradition of the Yellow Earth milieu. His second film, *Ju Dou*, was adapted from Liu Heng's novella *Fuxi Fuxi*. The story is set in the 1920s in a small remote town in Southern China, where life is rigid and governed by ancestral and familial precepts. Ju Dou is abused sexually and physically by her old crippled husband who owned a dye mill. She falls in love with her husband's nephew and has a boy with him although in the eyes of society and the law her crippled husband is the father of the boy. However, their infidelity is eventually discovered and then punished by their own son. Zhang's humanistic approach to cinema

---

2 The term 'Blue-Ocean civilisation' was used to characterize Western civilization in *River Elegy*, a documentary film broadcast on China Central Television (CCTV) in 1989. The film was regarded as one of the triggers to the Tiananmen student movement and banned due to its blunt political and cultural criticism and provocative language. The transcript of the documentary was translated into English and published by Cornell University Press.

enables him to reveal the inner struggle of these characters – their strong social and psychological burden, their desires for freedom, and their fears of breaking the established social conformity. Eventually conformity confines them to feudalistic family structures. His film is a syncretic presentation of realistic rural backwardness and idealistic human desires for freedom. Zhang is able to add artistic elements to the tragic story with romantic ambience. The setting of the dye mill provides bold colours as part of the visual language of the film, and the colourful dyed cloths fall and fold as the story 'unfolds'. His ability to employ many contrasting elements in the film ensures that the visual aesthetic remains significant throughout; for example, the colour red represents both the excitement of the secret love and the sacrifice of infidelity. *Ju Dou* was banned in China as the authorities deemed it unsuitable for Chinese audiences due to its sexual content and the explicit affair between a woman and her husband's nephew, which was traditionally considered incestuous in Chinese culture.

Raise the Red Lantern, based on the novella *Wives and Concubines* by Su Tong, is another 'writer's' movie directed by Zhang in 1991. It tells the story of a young college girl, Songlian, who is forced to become the fourth concubine of an old merchant by her stepmother after her father's death and how she manages to survive the scheming and backstabbing melee of wives and maids living under strict and highly traditional patriarchal rituals. The film depicts her life in the dark courtyard as wholly marked by loneliness, sorrow and despair. The title of this movie indicates a family ritual to signal the husband's sexual predilection and the illuminating red lantern, representing the hope and festivity in Chinese tradition, becomes a symbol of the suppressed life confined in the deep courtyard. The traditional courtyard, which is often filled with live activities and children, becomes a place enveloped with darkness and represents the closeness of the feudal society and the impasse of a stagnant life. Songlian and other wives and maids are stonewalled in this cruel and cold courtyard and, in different ways, they all become victims of family politics of power and control. Zhang deliberately constructs a narrative from each woman to reveal their sorrows and oppression; the film is thus a continuation of his themes on women and feudalistic oppression. He displays a full command of filmmaking technique in this film with his characteristic lighting and camera angles, especially his use of red lanterns, which, when contrasted to the dark-grey brick house and its rooftops, provides a detailed visual metaphor for the feudalistic ritual and the plight of women.

His three early films form a coherent discourse on national culture and identity, particularly the place of women in this tradition. Jiu'er in *Red Sorghum* expresses an idealistic and unrestrained, even wild, attitude and passion toward life, which is rarely found in Chinese characters; Ju Dou desires to break away from oppressive power structures; Songlian is distraught with the unjust oppression of the patriarchal system and is finally driven mad. Women thus occupy an important (and political) subject positioning in these films. They were also all released at a time when gender relations became quintessential emblems for the visual construction of filmmakers to define Chinese identity and culture for a transnational audience, especially among the fifth-generation filmmakers, as can also be seen in Chen Kaige's *Farewell My Concubine* (1993). Such motifs also continue in films made after this period which also examine gender and social issues in contemporary China. Together these films form a multi-dimensional narrative and discourse about women and gender issues in Chinese cinema.

However, Zhang and his films were accused of being too critical of Chinese culture and exposing negative social and cultural images. China's Film Bureau criticised his films for disclosing the darkness of Chinese culture to cater for foreign audiences and their tastes for exotic themes. In 1990, Teng Jinxian, director of the National Film Bureau, stated that some filmmakers are guilty of 'national nihilism' and blindly worship Western film theory and artistic genres. Such criticism reflects a rigid political and ideological control in art and literature in the period from 1989 to 1991. After the Tiananmen student movement in 1989, a political campaign against 'spiritual pollution' was launched to prevent art, literature and scholarly discussions from being influenced by Western and 'capitalist ideology'. Only films on moral-political educational themes, which bear the strong imprint of socialist realism, were endorsed by the government in order to promote patriotism; subsequently, *Ju Dou* and *Raise the Red Lantern* were forbidden to be shown in China. Scholars have argued that though censored closely by the Chinese authorities, the works of the fifth-generation of film directors have been recognised by Westerners for bringing the local to the global cultural arena, but also subtly catering to Westerners' racist impressions of the Chinese as a 'backward' people, with these directors' focus on 'primitive' nature and culture appealling to Western audiences (see Chow 1995; Lu 2001). Chinese critics further criticised his films for defying Chinese cultural identity and using women as erotic objects to appeal to Western audiences. To Zhang, however, his films simply enabled him to participate in the nation-wide dialogue on culture, tradition and modernity, and the international recognition they received internationalised that debate. His films have been highly acclaimed at international film festivals: *Red Sorghum* received the Golden Bear at the Berlin Film Festival in 1988; *Ju Dou* won the Luis Bruno Special Award at the Cannes Film Festival in 1990; *Raise the Red Lantern* won the Silver Lion at the Venice Film Festival and was nominated as best foreign language film at the Academy Awards in 1992.

In contrast to morbid stories of feudal oppression, it is noted that Zhang often brings exquisite visual display to his silver screen, forming his own distinctive aesthetic characteristics in his early films. Trained as cinematographer, Zhang stresses imagery, symbols, colours and angles, an artistic inspiration drawn from the cultural and social milieu where he grew up; bold colours such as red and yellow reflect the tradition of the Yellow Earth Plateau. This visual display of bold traditional colours suits the taste of transnational audiences, and the sheer 'visuality' of his films dramatises the plot and emotions of characters. For him, this was his major breakthrough in Chinese filmmaking and his later films carry similar artistic styles.

Second Stage: Discourse on Societal Change and Rural Life

If Zhang's early films intended to explore women's struggles against cultural boundaries and function as a visual construction of the national discourse on Chinese cultural history, his films later in the 1990s represent the discourses of social, economic and political life in rural China. His films at this stage are primarily concerned with the lives of the rural peasantry rather than the emerging urban middle class. He puts the lives of ordinary people under the spot light, including a young female village teacher, a village wife, a village girl and a rural family. *To Live* (1994) provides an interrogation of social changes in different eras of the communist regime; *The Story of Qiu Ju* (1992) and *Not One Less* (1997) expose social inequalities and injustices as the unanticipated consequences of the rapid economic reform. His films thus reveal the two faces of the economic development in contemporary China and express his concerns about social inequalities and injustice in China's countryside. Cinema, in Zhang's view, has social responsibilities for giving voice to underprivileged groups or at least providing a narration to their experiences; his films at this stage reflect the particular cinematic and literary interests in rural China. Similar themes are seen in other films produced at this time, including Zhou Xiaowen's *Ermo* (1994), the story of a rural woman who dreams of owning the largest television in her town. This is also a time that saw much academic and scholarly interest in rural China as sociologists and political scientists studied rural reform, village elections, poverty and other social issues.

To Live, based on the novel by Yu Hua, reveals the life of an ordinary family under turbulent political and social movements of communist China and their enduring hope for a quiet and peaceful life. It is in this film that Zhang started explicitly touching on political issues and movements, such as the Great Leap Forward and the Cultural Revolution. Similar to another film released in the same year, *The Blue Kite*, directed by another fifth-generation director Tian Zhuangzhuang, it alludes to the nation's political and social upheavals in the 1950s and 1960s. Both films use political events as background narratives and offer an intensely realistic portrayal of the shattered lives and hopes of innocent ordinary people; and not surprisingly both films were banned in China. Ironically, as the political content made these films un-screenable in China, it seemed to make them more acceptable and popular on the international film festival circuit as images of 'real' (in reality a highly exoticised) China.

The Story of Qiu Ju is another 'writer's movie', this time adapted from Chen Yuanbin's novel *Ten Thousand Litigations*. It is about a wife's perseverance to pursue social justice in a rural village. When Qiu Ju's husband is kicked in his groin by the village chief while they were bantering, she insists on an apology, but this never comes. The chief offers to pay the medical expenses but does not tender a verbal apology. She refuses this settlement and takes the case to the city, then to the capital. Eventually, she wins the case; however, when she sees the chief is arrested she appears to experience only loss and regret rather than relief or satisfaction. This film offers a glimpse of rural life in contemporary China, where law and justice is often entangled with hierarchical social relationship and bureaucracy. Compared with other female protagonists portrayed as victims of patriarchal suppression in Zhang's earlier films, Qiu Ju has the will and determination to fight for her own destiny; she breaks away from the bondage of community and hierarchy to seek social justice (even though in the end it seems to offer her little satisfaction). This film reveals multiple dimensions of rural life: it shows that saving face is still valued under the bureaucratic hierarchy, and probes the imperfect but subtle interfamilial and interpersonal relationship under imperfect social justice and law which is often governed by human relationship rather than legal contract. The film displays a strong realistic sentiment and empathy for Chinese peasantry and suggests that China's higher authorities are too far removed from the peasantry to protect them from the whims of local officials.

Not One Less takes a close look at issues of poverty and inequality in rural China where teachers are often unpaid or underpaid and parents do not have money to send school-age children to school. The film tells the story of a 13-year-old substitute teacher who tries to save a runaway student. She is determined to earn the additional pay promised if none of her 28 pupils becomes a dropout. When a mischievous ten-year-old vanishes, she goes to the nearby city to search for the elusive child. Unlike Zhang's other movies, *Not One Less* is filmed in a documentary style; further, it does not have contrasting colour themes and melodramatic stories as well as a glamorous cast. Zhang cast every role with nonprofessional actors 'playing' who they are in real life, lending authenticity and simplicity to the work.

This film exposes the contrasting differences between rural and urban life; it presents a realistic picture of children growing up in the countryside and the inadequate resources for public schooling. Even though their educational rights are protected under the 'nine-year compulsory education' law, poverty has limited educational opportunities and attainment. More critically, the film sends a message that such situations have been entirely overlooked in rural areas as the society at large moves fast towards modernity. Another Zhang film in this genre, *The Road Home* (2000), whose Chinese title would be translated as 'My Father and My Mother', carries a similar theme. This film, adapted from Bao Shi's novel *Remembrance*, starts with a city businessman Luo Yusheng returning to his home village for his father's funeral. On the day of the funeral more than a hundred of his father's former students come to carry the coffin. The film carries a sub-theme of how Yusheng finds his lost roots and values which are still cherished in the small village while he quests for social mobility and modernity in his urban mode of being.

These films show the formation of a strong sense of realism in Zhang's filmmaking career. Not only are the settings of his films true to life, but so too are the cast. These films express his humanistic sentiment about smaller-than-life figures and their social struggles which are heavily interlinked with the problems and issues of economic modernisation. Gender issues continue to be a central component, although whereas in previous films female suppression is the primary motif, women in his later socio-political films are portrayed as subjects fighting for their fates and destinies.

Joining the Mainstream: Market Pragmatism and Commercialism

The early 1990s was a critical time for the Chinese national film industry as it faced both internal and external challenges. Domestically, annual attendance at movie theatres dropped from 21 billion in 1982 to under 4.5 billion in 1991. Slow-pace artistic films offering a healthy dose of realism lost audiences and as a result failed to perform well at the box office. In 1994 the Chinese government decided to import ten big-hit Hollywood films each year.[3] As the Chinese audience became increasingly exposed to Hollywood films with big stars, big budgets and thrilling stories, Chinese filmmakers felt the pressure to seek for new directions for Chinese cinema. Zhang expressed his concerns that 'it is not only the fifth-generation filmmakers but all Chinese directors that should adapt to the trends of the era, and nurture the audience's interest in Chinese-made films' (in Yuankai 2003). For Zhang, the way to save the Chinese film industry was to create films that would seek to entertain rather than only educate the audience. His previous films had brought him international festival and academic recognition but had not

---

3　Hollywood films brought in huge box-office revenues, totalling about 75 per cent of all box-office revenue in 1995. Films imported in that year include *Natural Born Killers* (1994), *True Lies* (1994), *Toy Story* (1995), *Broken Arrow* (1995) and *Bridges of Madison County* (1995).

transformed into profit and market returns. For him, filmmaking had ceased to be about 'art' as a pure subject but rather about box office and the financial revenue that films bring in. This new direction has unsurprisingly brought Zhang accusations of compromising and complying with the Hollywood film model of pure entertainment and consumerism.

The film production system in China has also changed significantly since the mid-1980s. State-run studios were facing shortages of capital for film production as they could not solely depend on state funding any more. Investment from Hong Kong, Taiwan and foreign studios started flowing into the Chinese film industry; the overseas investors were particularly interested in filmmakers with successful box-office records, and they invested in experienced art and commercial filmmakers alike. The wooing of foreign film producers and studios via the pre-selling of overseas releasing rights has also become common. The fifth-generation filmmakers now had to develop a far greater awareness of how the international film market operated in order to succeed. Zhang Yimou, Tian Zhuangzhuang, Li Shaohong and Chen Kaige all began in this period to explore film projects with high levels of commercial potential. Box-office revenues and profit thus became the main impetus for the fifth-generation filmmakers in creating new work in the 1990s; capitalist economics has therefore greatly influenced the Chinese film industry since then, and changed the mentality of Chinese filmmakers who were committed to aesthetic principles to respond to popular demands for entertainment and economic pressures of the film industry to survive financially (see Zhu 2003).

Zhang's response to this challenge is to make films that can be seen to provide traditionally Hollywood-type ideals of 'entertainment' and 'action' rather than of purely artistic and social value. To break away from the early genres of his artistic flms, Zhang made several attempts to produce commercial entertaining movies in the mid-1990s. In 1995, he made a film about a Shanghai mafia based in the 1930s, *Shanghai Triad*, based on the novel *Family Rules* by Li Xiao. This film took much inspiration from older and highly successful Hong Kong gangster movies, and focuses on a beautiful woman (Gong Li) and her complicate relationship to various gang members. In 2000, he produced a romantic comedy, *Happy Times*, about a relationship between an aging unemployed bachelor and a chubby divorcée. Though this comedy explores some issues of contemporary Chinese society it lacks the soulfulness and artistry displayed in his previous movies.

The international success of Ang Lee's *Crouching Tiger, Hidden Dragon* (2000) gave Chinese filmmakers an answer in their search for an internationally successful film genre. Its award-winning performances at the Academy Awards and the Golden Globes indicated to Chinese directors that there was, and still is, a resurgent interest in martial arts movies in the West which had first seen popularity in the 1970s with the work of Bruce Lee (see Chan 2004: 3–7). This popularity inspired Western film studios and producers to show a renewed interest in this genre themselves.[4] However, the critical question for Chinese filmmakers was how to present a martial arts film with innovative storylines that maintained links with Chinese culture and the obligatory display of new CGI technology, as well as offering something that would appeal to both Western and Chinese audiences. Martial arts films are a clichéd but highly successful genre for Chinese filmmakers and audience; they started dominating the film market in the 1960s in Hong Kong with a series of films on Huang Feihong (or Wong Fei-Hung), and continued in mainland China in the early 1980s with a series of films on the Shaolin Temple.[5]

The first attempt that marks Zhang's transition from 'artistic' films to 'commercial' films is *Hero* (2002) and released in the West by Miramax Films. It was one of the most expensive Chinese films at that time with an budget of around $30 million, close to the $40 million investment of Chen Kaige's *The Promise* in 2005. The cast consisted of pan-Asian film stars, including Jet Li, Ziyi Zhang, Tony Leung and Maggie Cheung. The marketing campaign for the film was also unprecedented with a total of $5 million spent on publicity. Zhang's confidence in the appeal of the stars appeared to be correct with *Hero* receiving huge commercial success. It achieved record box-office sales in China with $30 million, $75 million in the US and $177 million worldwide.

---

4   The Weinstein bothers, founders of Miramax Films, have been involved with many highly acclaimed and financially successful Asian titles in the past, including Jet Li's *The Master* (1989), *Twin Warriors* (1993), *The Enforcer* (1995), *The Legend of the Swordsman* (1992), *The Legend* (1992), *The Legend II* (1993), *Fist of Legend* (1995) and *Shaolin Soccer* (2002). Sony Classics invested in Zhang Yimou's *House of Flying Daggers* (2004).
5   One of the first martial arts films, *Shaolin Temple*, starring Jet Li, was produced in 1982. Two sequels were produced in 1984 and 1986.

Hero represents Zhang's first attempt to shift from 'writer's movies' to an original script and Zhang served as the creator of the story as well as the director. This marks the decline of Zhang's film productions based on literary texts in order to pursue visuality and technical simulation, and martial arts films suit Zhang's artistic styles. In *Hero* he created a colourful poetic ambiance with the scenes of the red-dress fighting in the yellow foliage, black horses of the Qin cavalry, and the turquoise blue lake. Zhang aimed to integrate classical Chinese culture with martial arts aesthetics and action sequences. The film presents a new notion of being a hero: sacrificing personal interests, fame and missions in the search for social harmony and the common good. It redefines the concepts of swordsmanship, loyalty and honour.

Martial arts films have become Zhang's most economically successful genre and he produced three films in five years to form a loose trilogy. His second and third films in this mode, *House of Flying Daggers* and *Curse of the Golden Flower*, were released in 2004 and 2006 respectively. Differing from *Hero*'s strong motif of nationalism, *House of Flying Daggers* shows a strong influence of contemporary global youth culture with the focus on a love triangle among three good-looking protagonists. The common motif that permeats both *Hero* and *House of Flying Daggers* is sacrifice – the former is about the sacrifice of personal fame for the nation's well-being; the latter, sacrifice of life itself on the alter of true love. Though gaining wide international acclaim, *House of Flying Daggers* received negative comments from Chinese film critics and audiences for Zhang's clichéd filmmaking techniques and his apparent eagerness to please Western audiences. Further, his martial arts films are criticised as being devoid of innovation when compared to his early films or other martial arts films by Chinese or Hong Kong auteurs, and for 'using the same bucket … to draw different water' (*China Daily* 2004). The bamboo forest reminds audiences of the fight scene in a bamboo grove in *Crouching Tiger, Hidden Dragon* and the older Hong Kong film *Touch of Zen*, making the bamboo the quintessential icon of Chinese martial arts films and an uninspiring place to set another fight sequence. Even though scenes like the 'echo game', the battle in the lush green bamboo forest and the fight in the blizzard are highly pleasing on the eye, Chinese audiences found that the plot was too superficially complex and complained about the lack of development of suspense and the underwritten characters.

Such criticism applied to his latest film in this genre, *Curse of the Golden Flower*. Chinese critics felt it lacked a strong storyline and sophisticated dialogues (*China Daily* 2006). The primary source of the screenplay is a well-known Chinese classic play *Thunderstorm* by Cao Yu, set in the 1930s. Zhang re-wrote the story to set it in the Tang Dynasty, similar to *House of Flying Daggers*, and the narrative focuses on a power struggle amongst the emperor, the empress and three princes. To Chinese audiences and critics, it was just another film that intended to package Chinese culture with extravagant colours, heavily choreographed fighting scenes, costumes and palaces to appeal to a Western audience. It is a continuation of Zhang's intended effort to construct the image of China and export Chinese culture through cinema, but a shift from his early critical discourses on patriarchal culture to the imagined nostalgia of cultural nationalism as his martial arts films formulated the notion of a united China and the dynastic rule of the Qin and Tang. With a budget of $45 million, the film achieved total worldwide box-office sales of $92 million.

The trilogy of Zhang's martial arts films represent not only his effort to search for a new genre of filmmaking, but also a creative process during a significant transition period, or even compromise to the marketisation of China's film industry, and to the postmodern commercialism and consumerism taking place in China and the wider world. The three epic dramas represent the core of the mainstream Chinese entertainment industry and the recent surge of market obsession for epic narratives, which has been built up by Chinese TV dramas since the early 2000s as Chinese audiences are fascinated by palace politics, heroic figures and events in Chinese history. Chinese directors continue to work in this mode of production, of ancient costume films, epic martial art movies and history dramas, following Zhang and his classmates and contemporaries Chen Kaige's *The Promise* (2005) and Feng Xiaogang's *Night Banquet* (2006), a re-rendering of Shakespeare's *Hamlet*. This frenzy for epic drama and dynastic narratives also demonstrates audiences' nostalgic appetites for ancient history and culture as well as a quest for traditional values in contemporary Chinese society.

Zhang's martial arts films represent a postmodern globalised form of cultural products by virtue of their aesthetic rendering, means of production, market operation, global reach of their distribution networks, and transnational audiences. All three films are the products of a global production team. For instance, in *House of Flying Daggers*, the original theme music is composed and produced by Japanese musician Shigeru Umebayashi, the theme song is performed by American singer Kathleen Battle, and the costume is designed by Emi Wada from Japan. All films were cast with pan-Asian stars from Hong Kong (Tony Leung, Maggie Cheung, Chow Yun-Fat and Andy Lau), Taiwan (Jay Chou and Takeshi Kaneshiro) and mainland China (Jet Li, Zhang Ziyi and Gong Li). Sources of funding for these films were multinational too; *Hero* was funded by Beijing New Picture and Elite Group Enterprises in Hong Kong. Miramax released this film beyond China and Quentin Tarantino, who is well recognised for his interest in and broad knowledge (and perhaps his continual plagiarism) of Chinese cinema, actively worked with Zhang and Miramax to 'introduce' *Hero* to Western audiences. *House of Flying Daggers* was produced by Edko Films (Hong Kong) and Zhang Yimou Studio in collaboration with Beijing New Picture and Elite Group, and released in the US by Sony Pictures Classics. Even the plots of the films are symbolic of the global cultural hybrid: *House of Flying Daggers* bears a similar storyline to the plot of the Hong Kong film *Internal Affairs* (2002), on which Martin Scorsese's *The Departed* (2006) is also based. *Curse of the Golden Flower* alludes to the Chinese stage play *Thunderstorm* as well as several Shakespeare tragedies with the three siblings from *King Lear*, the jealous king from *Othello*, the scheming queen of *Macbeth*, and the carnage in the palace of *Hamlet*. *House of Flying Daggers* blends a contemporary romantic narrative into Chinese costumes.

Traditionally, martial arts films carry the burden and responsibility of cultural representation. Such cultural missions have been shown in Zhang's early films and can be seen in his new films – albeit in a more commercial format. His new films focus on visual expression with splendid colours and computer-aided imagery. As Zhang felt the challenge was how to find a niche to integrate Chinese cultural tradition with the taste of Western audiences, he heavily incorporated Chinese cultural symbols in his films. In *Hero*, Chinese calligraphy was shown to have nineteen different ways to write the word 'sword'. In *House of Flying Daggers*, the scenes of 'autumn birch forest', 'snow fields' and 'Peony Pavilion' resemble the beauty of ancient Chinese ink-and-water landscape paintings. Zhang repeatedly demonstrates his ability to use splendid colours and the natural landscapes to appeal to transnational audiences, and this strategy was certainly successful. These three films received widespread acclaim and many awards at international film festivals. *Hero* was nominated for the Best Foreign Language Film at the 2003 Academy Awards and received the Alfred Bauer Award at the Berlin International Film Festival in 2003. *Curse of the Golden Flowers* was nominated for the Best Achievement in Costume Design at the 2007 Academy Awards. However, Zhang's eagerness to show Chinese cultural elements to the Western audience makes his martial arts films largely failed attempts to break away from what has become an almost clichéd and predictable filmmaking style.

Zhang has become a savvy businessman operating in the global film industry. He orchestrates complex marketing campaigns for his films, and releases news and pictures constantly during the production process through various types of mass media, thus seeing these movies become the talk of the whole nation. He staged a $6 million grand gala for the worldwide premier of *Curse of the Golden Flower* and a concert full of movie and music stars, which was broadcast across the nation in 2006 (*People's Daily* 2007). To expand the commercial impact of these movies, Zhang also sold the rights to writers to write stories, and game developers to develop online games based on these films – certainly reminiscent of *The Matrix* franchise and the way many productions are now maximising their films incomes through other forms of new media.

Similar patterns of postmodern cultural productions are found in his artistic creations beyond the cinematic circuit. With the international capital flows into Chinese art, film and other cultural industries, China's intellectuals and artists have changed their roles in defining national identity and culture in an era of postmodern globalisation (see Lu 2001: 45). Zhang continues to look for ways to define Chinese culture via artistic productions beyond cinema and to connect popular culture, regional culture, national culture and transnational capital to create profit-driven cultural productions. In the last ten years he has expanded his career into other diverse areas. In 1998 he signed a contract with Michael Ecker's company, Opera on Original Site, to produce Puccini's *Turandot* at the Forbidden City in Beijing. With a $15 million budget Zhang incorporated Chinese elements into the Italian opera, including drum corps, Ming-dynasty costumes, palace stage setting, martial arts, ghost figures and the Imperial red and gold colours. Zhang also made his debut at the Metropolitan Opera in New York City in 2007 by directing the world premiere of Tan Dun's opera, *The First Emperor*, a sequel to his movie *Hero* on China's Qin Emperor. These opera productions represent Zhang's efforts to present China and Chinese culture to transnational audiences at global stages.

His artistic and cultural productions at regional levels in China are also highly visible. Since 2004 Zhang has produced three landscape musicals (*shijing ju*), which are often referred to as the Impression series, in Yangshuo, Lijiang and in West Lake, Hangzhou. The rise of cultural consumerism has engendered the creation of new cultural representations of regional cultures in southern China. Funded by local governments and supported by a Hong Kong firm with the purpose of promoting local culture as well as tourism, these landscape musicals provide visual presentation of the regional sub-culture to tourists. The outdoor landscape musicals represent the emergence of southern cultures as the result of the regional economic prosperity in southern China and the corresponding search for regional cultures. Besides these, he staged a ballet based on his film *Raise the Red Lantern* for the National Ballet Troupe. In 2008 Zhang was the director of the dramatic Beijing Olympic Games opening and closing ceremonies.

Zhang's engagements in these art projects demonstrate versatility in his artistic endeavours outside film industry. Though these projects show his artistic aspiration and imagination, they also reveal his commercial pragmatism. He is concerned more about market value and recognition, and is criticised for letting fame take precedence over art and losing his edge of cultural and social criticism as exhibited in his early films.

Zhang Yimou and Future Generations of Chinese Filmmakers

Zhang represents the quintessential fifth-generation filmmaker in China. His career trajectory has taken him from the art film studio to the mainstream of the international film industry. In the early 1980s, when Zhang and his classmates graduated from Beijing Film Academy, they had little knowledge about the 'market'. What concerned them most was the artistic value and humanistic expression of their films. The rise of pop culture and consumerism has driven the Chinese film industry and filmmakers to become more market-oriented, profit-driven and pragmatic as a consequence of the compromise to the market economy. Zhang's own filmmaking in the last two decades shows a journey from challenging artistic work to more entertaining films and his conformity to the Hollywood entertainment industry; he has become an art entrepreneur and capitalist with a strong sense of commercial pragmatism in his artistic productions. However, a new group of Sixth-Generation and Seventh-Generation Chinese filmmakers have emerged and their films show a reburgeoning interest in humanistic films about cultural, social and human struggles in the era of economic modernisation. Born in the 1970s, they are concerned with streetscapes and cityscapes. Their films intend to show urban struggles and desires, displaying a strong humanism and a blunt political attitude. Leading members of this group include Zhang Yuan (*Beijing Bastards*, 1992; *East Palace West Palace*, 1996; *Seventeen Years*, 1999), Zhang Yang (*Shower*, 1999), Wang Xiaoshuai (*Beijing Bicycle*, 2001) and Li Yang (*Blind Shaft*, 2003). Though they are not as influential as their Fifth-Generation counterparts, their humanistic films have imposed challenges to the older generation of filmmakers. This is a challenge that Zhang seems to be prepared to accept since in the last five years he has created a remarkable range of films. His 2005 film *Riding Alone for Thousands of Miles* shows a return to his earlier style of focusing on humanistic values and everyday life in the heart warming tale of an elderly Japanese man (Japanese star Takakura Ken) who travels to China to try to gain his son's forgiveness. *Under a Hawthorne Tree* (2010) returned the time of the Cultural Revolution. The film was an adaption of popular 2007 novel *Hawthorn Tree Forever* by Ai Mi and examines the doomed relationship between a teenage student and an older man. In 2009 Zhang remade the Coen Brothers noir hit *Blood Simple* (1985) into the screwball comedy thriller *A Woman, a Gun and a Noodle Shop*. His forthcoming feature (at the time of writing) *13 Flowers of Nanjing* (due for release in 2012) visits the traumatic and controversial topic of the Nanjing Massacre. With American star Christian Bale confirmed as the lead and with a reported $90million budget, Zhang continues to demonstrate the power he wields as a director and a producer on the global film circuit. The critical question for both audiences and the film industry has always been what Zhang will do next in his film career.

Bibliography

Bourdieu, Pierre (1990) *The Logic of Practice*, trans. Richard Nice. Stanford, CA: Stanford University Press.

Chan, Kenneth (2004) 'The Global Return of the Wu Xia Pian (Chinese Sword-Fighting Movie): Ang Lee's Crouching Tiger, Hidden Dragon', *Cinema Journal*, 43, 4, Summer, 3–17.

Chen, Yuanbin (1991) 'Wanjia susong' ['Ten Thousand Litigations'], Xiao-shuo yuebao [Short Story Monthly], 8, 2–33.

China Daily (2004) 'House of Flying Daggers Fails to Draw Much Blood', 21 July.

China Daily (2006) 'Ways of looking at *Curse of the Golden Flower*', 15 December.

Chow, Rey (1995) *Primitive Passions: Visuality, Sexuality, Ethnography, and Contemporary Chinese Cinema*. New York: Columbia University Press.

Heng, Liu (1988) 'Fuxi Fuxi', in Wang Ziping and Li Tuo (eds) *Zhongguo xiaoshuo* [Chinese Fiction]. Hong Kong: Sanlian shudian, 80–171.

Huang, Ray (1997) *China: A Macro History*. New York: M. E. Sharpe.

Lu, Sheldon (2001) *China, Transnational Visuality, Global Postmodernity*. Stanford, CA: Stanford University Press.

People's Daily (2007) 'Zhang Yimou's Curse of Golden Flower to premiere in China', 15 December.

Shaogong, Han (1986) 'Wenxue de Gen,' Miandui kongkuo er shenmi de shijie [Facing the Wide and Mysterious World]. Hangzhou, China: Zhejiang wenyi chubanshe.

Tong, Su (2004) *Raise the Red Lantern*. New York: Harper Perennial.

Yan, Mo (1994) *The Red Sorghum: A Story of China*. New York: Penguin.

Yuankai, Tang (2002) 'Fifth-Generation Filmmakers Advance Towards the Market', *China Today*, June. Available at: http://www.chinatoday.com.cn/English/e20026/film.htm (accessed June 2003).

Yu, Hua (2003) *To Live: A Novel*. New York: Anchor-Random House.

Yutang, Lin (1998) *The Importance of Living*. New York: Harper.

Zhu, Ying (2003) *Chinese Cinema During the Era of Reform: The Ingenuity of the System*. Westport, CN: Praeger.

Feng Xiaogang and Ning Hao: Directing China's New Film Comedies

J. Colleen Berry

Although in most countries the existence and availability of film comedy is taken for granted, it has been a rarity in post-1949 China. Hong Kong is well known for its film comedies, but only in the last decade or so has China begun to produce film comedy.[1] Due primarily to the remarkable changes in the economy which have produced the dramatic economic upturn that China has been enjoying, and the concurrent changes in governmental stipulations on what is and is not politically acceptable, comedy has been making something of a comeback in Chinese film. Two relatively new directors, in particular, are leading the way in the box-office success of Chinese film comedy: Feng Xiaogang and Ning Hao. While Feng has been making films since at least 2000 that have been box-office hits and is regarded by many within China as China's third best-known director after Zhang Yimou and Chen Kaige (see *China Daily* 2007), Ning has appeared on the scene even more recently, propelled into the limelight by his 2006 comedy, *Crazy Stone*.

Here I will first contextualise these two directors by providing a brief overview of the ideological changes related to art in China over the past

---

1   There were certainly comedic elements in earlier films such as Huang Jianxin's satiric *Black Cannon Incident* (*Hei pao shijian*, 1986) and in Zhang Yimou's *The Story of Qiu Ju* (1992) and *To Live* (1994), but there were no full-blown major film comedies that achieved box-office success prior to the mid-1990s.

twenty to thirty years, and the changes in the production and distribution of Chinese film. I will then discuss the two directors, Feng Xiaogang and Ning Hao, in terms of what makes their works significant, why their comedies work, and what they reveal about contemporary Chinese society and identity.

Background: No Laughing Matter

First we need to look into the issue of why there has been such a dearth of film comedy until recently. In the past, there have been numerous attempts to explain the relative lack of a 'Chinese' sense of humour and how it may or may not differ from that of a non-Chinese sense of humour. One of these early articles focused on the relative newness of the concept of humour or *youmo*, a cognate created from the sounds of the English word and coined by the well known Chinese scholar, Lin Yutang (1885–1976), to demonstrate that 'humour' is a Western concept that is relatively new in China (see Hu 2005). Another essay attributes the lack of humour to Confucian attitudes about face and its strict injunctions to maintain one's dignity (see Xu 2004). C. T. Hsia differentiates between satire and humour and he concludes that the laughter of the Chinese masses has remained at a rather 'immature' level and has not advanced into the stage of humour. He sees China as a land of 'rich unconscious humour' and claims that 'the average Chinese enjoys various forms of ridicule and laughter which do not have the dignity or charity of humour' (Hsia 1978).

However persuasive these arguments may have been in the past, they are not longer relevant: a fact made abundantly clear by a viewing of Feng's and Ning's comedies. Moreover, I would argue that the primary reason for the lack of filmic comedy in post-1949 China lies in the political and economic spheres rather than in the philosophical or psychological. Seven years before the founding of the Peoples Republic of China, Mao Zedong declared at the 1942 Yenan Forum on Arts and Literature that the arts and literature were to be used in service to the people (referring mainly to the workers, peasants and soldiers) and to advance the revolution; writers were to restrict what they wrote and not 'make the mistake of ridiculing them [the people]' (Mao 1967: 70). This idea that art was meant to serve the people and not make fun of them remained intact for decades. An extension of Mao's dictates on the arts was that film, like all the arts, should convey a positive image of and to society, provide role models and legitimate the messages, actions and role of the government. Comedy, in particular, was regarded as frivolous, pointless, subversive and damaging in its ability to satirise and ridicule its targets. Even the traditionally irreverent form of indigenous Chinese comedy, 'crosstalk' (*xiangsheng*) has been domesticated and confined to 'safer' topics (see Moser 2004).

On the economic front, until recently, China has struggled. The widespread starvation brought on by the Great Leap Forward and the chaos into which China was plunged during the decade of the Cultural Revolution (1966–76) which took a toll on the Chinese economy. China's troubles internally and externally were no laughing matter. The vast majority of citizens had little extra time or money and the dire conditions that China was experiencing did not provide much fodder for humour and laughter. Moreover, under these circumstances, the government was far more interested in using the arts to promote socialism and to further the aims of the revolution than in providing entertainment.

However, especially since the early 1990s, China has undergone tremendous changes in virtually every area – political, economic, social and cultural. The government has become less intrusive in people's daily lives and as a result there has been a dramatic change in the fine arts, literature and cinema. Sex, for example, once taboo, has become a ubiquitous and highly visible presence in almost all the arts. While I certainly am not claiming that there are no restrictions or that censorship is dead, by comparison with earlier times there is a much higher degree of openness and of artistic freedom. As long as filmmakers and other artists stay within the relatively broad confines of what the government feels is acceptable, their works are not heavily censored. Of course, the problem remains of determining where exactly those lines are drawn.

This more tolerant political climate is both a product and a cause of China's booming economy. In order to attract foreign investment, China has had to open its door far wider than ever before. More foreign investment has meant a huge increase in the foreign tourists and in the numbers of expatriates living in China's major cities, especially Beijing and Shanghai, who are free to interact with Chinese citizens. Furthermore, the role that the Internet has played in connecting many more Chinese citizens directly with the outside world cannot be underestimated. In addition, there are a great number of Chinese students studying in other countries; they naturally become very familiar with life in those countries and when they come back to China to visit or to live they share what they have experienced with their friends and families in China.

Another factor in the re-emergence of Chinese film comedy has been, ironically, the widespread availability of pirated editions of both Chinese and foreign films. Because of the affordability of these DVDs for middle-class Chinese, Chinese audiences have become highly film-literate and able to understand intertextual references to other films. And, for the filmmakers themselves, media piracy means that they have had unfettered access to the films being made by their counterparts outside China. Wu Hao, a documentary filmmaker, also adds that the legitimate or non-pirated DVDs are subject to censorship and it is only through the pirated copies that viewers can see the original, uncut versions (Wu 2006).

Finally, there has been a transition from the complete monopoly on the production and distribution of films by the government to the emergence of films created, produced and distributed with the backing of private Chinese and foreign investment. This has meant a sea change in terms of the kinds of films being produced in China. Under the state monopoly up to the early 1980s, Chinese cinema was primarily used to promote governmental policies and promulgate Marxist socialist ideology. The films, like the model operas of Jiang Qing (Mao's wife) that were produced during the Cultural Revolution, were didactic, melodramatic works. During the early 1970s, opera and film had to adhere to the dictates of Jiang who promoted the principle of the 'three prominences' which meant that every work had to feature a number of 'positive characters', and among these, the focus was to be on a smaller group of 'heroic characters', the most prominent of which should be the principle hero. The heroes (strong, upright socialist-type revolutionaries) and villains (characters that worked against the collective, revolutionary good) stood in stark contrast to one another and good always triumphed over evil.

A little more than a decade after the Cultural Revolution ended, the so-called 'Fifth Generation' directors began releasing films that would revolutionise Chinese cinema both in China and abroad.[2] These films, most representative of which are the early films of Chen Kaige (*Yellow Earth* (1984), *Farewell My Concubine* (1993)) and Zhang Yimou (*Red Sorghum* (1987), *Ju Dou* (1990), *Raise the Red Lantern* (1991)), signalled a radical departure from the previous types of government-sponsored socialist films. Besides their stunning cinematography, the films of the Fifth Generation directors were far more human-centred and ambiguous in regard to the role of the Chinese Communist Party and its ideology. They won numerous international film awards but were criticised within the country as portraying an exoticised, sexual China that pandered to the way the West viewed the country. A number of these films were banned in China but even those that were allowed to play in Chinese theatres were criticised for being too dense and not entertaining enough for the ordinary Chinese viewer to appreciate.

With the advent of foreign investment came a loosening in state control of film production and distribution. The state relinquished its monopoly and private companies, both domestic and foreign, began to play an increasingly larger role. This move away from a state-owned and -operated production and distribution system to private companies whose aims were not ideological but financial led to the commercialisation of film and to the 'genre' film such as the 'New Years Comedy' (*hesui pian*) that has become virtually synonymous with the name of Feng Xiaogang (see Kong 2007).

Feng Xiaogang: Seriously Funny

Feng Xiaogang, a Beijing native, started out not as a graduate of the prestigious Beijing Film Academy or any other film institute but as a self-taught stage designer in the army. From there, he went on to work as an art designer for television dramas. Taking what he learned from his experiences in the television world, he was able to gain some experience as a screenwriter and was even given the chance to do a bit of directing. From there, he made his bid to branch out and make his own movies.

---

2   The term 'Fifth Generation' is somewhat ambiguous but, in general, it refers to directors who belonged to the first class to graduate in 1982 from the Beijing Film Academy when it reopened after being closed for the duration of the Cultural Revolution.

Feng has been a writer, producer, production designer and actor, but he is best known as a director. His directorial debut was in 1994 with the film *Gone Forever with My Love* (*Yong shi wo ai*). However, it was not until he released his first so-called 'New Year comedy' that his name became a household word. These New Year comedies became his most successful vehicle for the films that followed.

New Year comedies are films so named because their release coincides with the period of time between the end of December and the lunar New Year which falls between late January and mid-February. The purpose of these films is to stimulate consumer consumption and Feng's movies have proven extremely useful in this regard (see Kong 2007: 229). The first in this series of hits was *Dream Factory* (*Jiafang, Yifang*) in 1997, followed by *Be There or Be Square* (*Bujian busan*) the next year. In 2001 he co-wrote and directed *Big Shot's Funeral* which starred Donald Sutherland along with the well-known Chinese actor Ge You (a friend of Feng who has had a lead role in most of his films), Paul Mazursky, and Hong Kong actor Rosamund Kwan. Feng continued to make highly successful low-budget comedies until 2004 when he switched gears and moved into the drama genre with *A World Without Thieves*. That film caught the attention of the outside world and in 2004 Feng was named one of the 'Opinion Shapers' in *Business Week* magazine's twenty-five 'Stars of Asia', a list that included policy makers, entrepreneurs, corporate managers and financiers.

Regardless of the type of film Feng makes, he has stated repeatedly that his goal is to make movies that appeal to his audiences. And, despite his huge popularity in China, before *A World Without Thieves* won a Golden Horse for the best screenplay adaptation, he was not an award-winning director. While he does not claim to be oblivious to his critics, he makes no apologies about making films for the commercial market. He told an interviewer: 'I'm trying to ensure that the audience gets the most fun and inspiration from the screen. But I would never make a movie to win an award' (*China Daily* 2004).

Regardless of his intentions, Feng Xiaogang's films are far from mindless commercial fare. His comedies as well as his recent dramas deal with serious issues in contemporary urban Chinese society. He lampoons the pretentious, status-conscious, emerging middle class: 'I like to satirise the people who are pretentious and self-important, who think they're on a higher level than everyone else … There's a new group of people emerging in China who are rich and want to live a Western sort of lifestyle. I find that ridiculous and funny, because I don't think it's compatible with being in China' (Elmer 2008).

In the film *Cell Phone* (2003), Feng stirs up problems for married men who use their cell phones to communicate with their lovers and are caught by their wives. As a result of the film, the phrase 'I'm in a meeting' has become a red flag for women who are suspicious of their partner's activities. *Big Shot's Funeral*, a full-out comedy, takes aim at greed and the over-the-top production by the sponsors of what is supposed to be a funeral for an American movie director who wants it to be a comedy. *Be There or Be Square* pokes fun at the Chinese obsession with emigrating to the US; it centres around the lives of two Beijing natives who have become illegal immigrants in Los Angeles. *A Sigh* (2000) tackles the issue of extramarital relationships and the price paid both by those involved in the affair and their families.

Feng's humour is often quite dark and satirical; much of it is not readily apparent to viewers unfamiliar with either the language or the conditions in contemporary Chinese society. Critics of his more recent films such as *A World Without Thieves*, *The Banquet* (2006) and *Assembly* (2007) have claimed that he is now trying to capture an international audience and hoping that he will become as well known outside China as he is within the country, but it may also be that he is expanding his field and challenging himself with new genres. Despite the fact that he sees himself as a commercial filmmaker whose goal is to entertain his viewers, Feng is an auteur, a serious filmmaker whose style is imprinted upon all the films he directs.

Ning Hao: Laughing all the way to the Box Office

Ning Hao, one of the newest – and youngest – faces in Chinese film comedy, set up his own studio, the Ning Hao Film Studio, in 2003 and has already produced a number of award-winning films. His first four films – *Thursday, Wednesday* (*Xingqisi, Zingqisan*, 2001), *Incense* (*Xianghuo*, 2003), *Mongolian Ping Pong* (*Lü caodi*, 2005) and *Crazy Stone* (*Fengkuang de shitou*, 2006) – were all nominated for and won numerous prizes including international film festival awards. It was the wildly popular comedy, *Crazy Stone*, however, that propelled Ning Hao into both the domestic and international spotlight.

Although *Crazy Stone* is Ning's biggest hit, it is not likely to be his last. His film *Silver Medalist* (2009) and another project in the works *7 Dreams* both won the backing of the Hong Kong Asia Film Financing Forum, an organisation that connects Asian filmmakers with various internationally known financial backers. This recognition and the funding that comes with it demonstrate Ning's growing stature as a director and the seriousness with which his projects are being taken.

What is it that caused *Crazy Stone* to attract such a huge audience of fans? Like Feng Xiaogang, Ning Hao claims that his primary interest is in entertaining his audiences. He used all the colours in his director's palate to paint his comedic masterpiece, *Crazy Stone*: a host of characters that parody certain types found on the margins of society; music that runs the gamut from C-pop to Beijing opera to *Swan Lake*; settings like bathrooms, a rundown factory and a dirt-cheap flophouse – all familiar in daily life but not generally portrayed in Chinese films; a well-off-the-beaten-track location (Chongqing) and its local dialect; and frenetic camerawork that overlaps scenes and jumps both ahead and behind the events presented, mimicking the confusing, rapidly changing physical and cultural environment.

Ning also incorporates three layers of comedy that work together to make the film appeal to foreign as well as Chinese audiences. The layer that is most easily understood by any audience is that of physical comedy. Even viewers without an understanding of contemporary Chinese culture or language can appreciate the fast pace of the film, the vaudeville slapstick and mayhem and the general goofiness of most of the characters. The handheld videocam cinematography and the diverse musical score add to this layer of comedy which depends more on the eyes and ears than the brain to make people laugh.

The second layer is the 'global' comedy which includes parody and the 'borrowing' of scenes from other films. Audiences that are film literate can readily appreciate the references to other films and Ning pays homage to a number of non-Chinese films in *Crazy Stone*, most notably *Mission Impossible I* (Brian DePalma, 1996), *Lock, Stock and Two Smoking Barrels* (Guy Ritchie,

1998) and *Snatch* (Guy Ritchie, 2000). Some of the scenes seem to pay homage to Quentin Tarantino, who is quoted on the *Crazy Stone* DVD cover as saying, 'I'm happy to love a movie this much.' Therefore, even when an audience consists solely of Chinese viewers watching the film in China, it is still a 'global' audience because the viewers can appreciate the intertextual references and parodies of films made outside China.

'Global' comedy includes not only references to other films, but to any modern trend that a globally savvy audience would be familiar with or have experience of. Technology is one such area: in *Crazy Stone*, as in Feng Xiaogang's *Cell Phone*, the high-tech falls prey to low-tech or even to itself and causes endless headaches for the owner. High-tech gadgets are shown as being unreliable, frivolous diversions – impediments rather than aids that are even dangerous in the wrong hands. Cell phones, for example, often fail to work when they are most needed: in one scene in *Crazy Stone*, a thief is trapped in a sewer tunnel but when he tries to use his cell phone to call for help, he is out of range and unable to pick up a signal – and his battery is almost dead. Later, we are shown an antenna poking out of one of the holes in the manhole cover as he tries to catch the signal.

Finally, Ning adds 'local' comedy to the mix of comedic elements. By local comedy, I am referring to those aspects of the film that appeal especially to the sense of humour of a Chinese-speaking audience and which are a familiar part of contemporary culture in the PRC. This term is not limited merely to comedy that appeals to or is comprehensible to Chinese viewers in China or even to those from a Chinese cultural background who are living outside of China; rather, it indicates a type of humour that would be understandable (and funny) to anyone who has the knowledge of the languages and local conditions within China. This understanding of the local conditions within China, and especially in the part of China where the film takes place, allows the viewer to 'get' the local comedy. Therefore, an audience who understands the local comedy could include viewers outside as well as inside China.

Because *Crazy Stone* is Ning Hao's first and only major success, it is difficult to ascribe auteur status to him at this point, but if he continues to apply the same creativity and range of skills to his future films, he will no doubt be considered one of China's foremost directors.

Ning and Feng: Keeping it 'Chinese'

Ning and Feng have hit pay dirt through the use of local comedy and the targets they satirise. Of the three registers of humour found in their films, it is the local comedy that makes their films so appealing to domestic audiences. Both directors have deliberately tried to make their films more 'Chinese' in order to attract Chinese viewers. In a post-production interview on the *Crazy Stone* DVD, Ning states that he and the other screenwriters had to go to great pains to rework the screenplay to make it more 'Chinese' after the original draft was criticised for being too much like a Hong Kong or foreign film ('Interview...', 2006).[3] Two elements that he felt were very important in making a more 'Chinese' film were the location for the film (Chongqing), and the characters, which he wanted to model on the *laobaixing*, the common people. Ning Hao describes *Crazy Stone*: 'It's about the reality of this crazy developing China and Chongqing being a microcosm of the country ... In this crazy city, there must be a lot of crazy stories' (*China Daily* 2006).

We can see examples of local comedy that the ordinary Zhou can relate to in the stereotypical characters found in contemporary Chinese society that Ning ridicules: rich but unethical real estate developers; poor but hardworking, responsible employees; 'sophisticated' outsiders; those extravagant spendthrifts, the nouveau riche; spoiled rich kids who are the unintended by-product of the one-child-per-family policy; the ubiquitous *liumang* or petty criminals; and the country-bumpkin labourers who come to the city to find work. Feng also satirises the pretentious rich or those who try to pass themselves off as wealthy or connected. For example, in *Big Shot's Funeral*, he makes fun of a self-important promoter whose grandiose ideas are nothing short of ridiculous.

Another aspect of local comedy that both directors employ is the use of language and dialect. For example, the primary language in *Crazy Stone* is not the standard language of China, Mandarin, but Chongqing dialect – a dialect as funny (and incomprehensible) to many northern Mandarin-speaking viewers as Brad Pitt's 'gypsy' English in *Snatch* is, or the accent

---

3   Ironically, despite this criticism, the very low-budget film got a big break when Hong Kong superstar Andy Lau decided to help out by backing it with funds from his Asia New Director Project.

of the characters in *Fargo* (Coen Brothers, 1996) to many native English speakers. Feng uses both the Sichuan and the Hebei dialect to comic effect in *Cell Phone* and *A World Without Thieves*, respectively. In the latter, he also juxtaposes slick, quick-talking cosmopolitan characters with a simple, rustic country boy from Hebei whose heavily accented Mandarin accentuates his naive pronouncements on honesty and human nature (see Lu 2007).

The use of English in *Crazy Stone*, and by extension, the Chinese who speak it, particularly those in or from Hong Kong, is also the target of ridicule. One of the characters, an ineffectual spoiled son of a factory owner, attempts to sound cultured by using an English name; he always introduces himself to the women he is trying to pick up by saying casually in Chinese, 'My name is Xie Xiaomeng. Just call me Charles.' This comes across as funny because it is part of the character's unsuccessful attempt to portray himself as an urban sophisticate. 'Charles', we are informed, had lived in Hong Kong where it is common practice for Chinese people to use English names. However, his efforts to transplant this aspect of Hong Kong culture and his adoption of it into the context of the urban jungle of the 'more Chinese' Chongqing are laughable.

In *A World Without Thieves* the study of English is the vehicle that launches the plot – a businessman studying English becomes sexually attracted to his tutor who encourages his desires in order to extort money from him. Just as in *Crazy Stone*, English is associated with pretentiousness and materialism.

The success of the comedies of Ning Hao and Feng Xiaogang are intimately connected to the way they satirise contemporary Chinese culture. Although what makes a film 'Chinese' has become almost impossible to pinpoint due to its transnational nature, the film comedies of Ning and Feng have a distinctly and deliberate Chinese flavour. Unlike many of the exotic-China art films of their Fifth Generation predecessors, Ning's and Feng's works are set in a modern, technologically savvy China where rampant materialism and ostentatious displays of wealth and status provide plenty of fodder for comedy.

The growing prominence, both within and outside China, of new filmmakers like Feng Xiaogang and Ning Hao, both of whom are best known for their film comedies, reflect a trend in the Chinese entertainment world that is not likely to end anytime soon. 'China has a feeling for entertainment, as America does', Ning explains. 'It shows that Chinese people do want to consume Chinese culture and aren't just satisfied consuming McDonald's' (*China Daily* 2006). The key to their success as directors lies in their skilful combination of local elements based in a Chinese cultural and physical environment with global elements borrowed from, or that parody, Western cinema. Moreover, their films have appeared at a time when China is enjoying a burgeoning economy and a renewed sense of confidence in its present and future – all factors which must make it easier to laugh, even at itself.

Bibliography

China Daily (2004) 'Feng Xiaogang's New New Year Plan'. Online. Available at: http://www.chinadaily.com.cn/english/doc/2004-12/08/content_398333.htm (accessed 8 December 2004).

____ (2006) 'Young Director's Heist Flick Steals Chinese Hearts'. *China Daily*. Online. Available at: http://www.chinadaily.com.cn/cndy/2006-08/10/content_661192.htm (accessed 10 August 2006).

____ (2007) 'Feng Xiaogang: The People's Filmmaker'. Online. Available at: http://www.china.org.cn/english/entertainment/221742.htm (accessed 22 August 2007).

Elmer, David (2008) 'Feng Xiaogang Has the West in His Sights with Assembly. *Times Online*. Available at: http://entertainment.timesonline.co.uk/tol/arts_and_entertainment/film/article3448182.ece> (accessed 2 March 2008).

Hsia, C. T. (1978) 'The Chinese Sense of Humor', *Renditions*, 9, Spring. From an unpublished manual on China written in 1953. Online. Available at: http://www.renditions.org/renditions/sps/s_9.html (accessed 20 February 2008).

Hu, Ping (2005) 'Do the Chinese Have a Sense of Humor?', *Association for Asian Research*. Online. Available at: http://www.asianresearch.org/articles/2561.html. (accessed 1 February 2008).

'Interview with the Director, Ning Hao' (2006) (supplementary material on DVD release of *Crazy Stone*). DVD. Focus Films and Warner China Film HG Corporation.

Kong, Shuyu (2007) 'Genre Film, Media Corporations, and the Commercialisation of the Chinese Film Industry: The Case of "New Year Comedies"', *Asian Studies Review*, 31, 3, 227–42.

Lu, Sheldon (2007) 'Dialect and Modernity in 21st Century Sinophone Cinema', *Jump Cut: A Review of Contemporary Media*, 49, Spring. Online. Available at: http://www.

ejumpcut.org/currentissue/Lu/index.html (accessed 8 December 2004).

Mao, Zedong (1967) 'Talks at the Yenan Forum on Literature and Art', in *Selected Works of Mao Tse-tung*. Vol. 3. Peking: Foreign Languages Press, 69-97.

Moser, David (2004) 'Stifled Laughter: How the Communist Party Killed Chinese Humor', *Danwei*, 16 November. Online. Available at: http://www.danwei.org/tv/stifled_ laughter_how_the_commu.php> (accessed 1 February 2008).

Wu, Hao (2006) 'In Defense of Piracy', *NPR: Marketplace*. Online. Available at:http:// marketplace.publicradio.org/display/web/2006/01/19/in_defense_of_piracy (accessed 19 January 2006).

Xu, Weihe (2004) 'The Confucian Politics of Appearance – and Its Impact on Chinese Humor', *Philosophy East and West*, 54, 4, October, 514–32.

Filmography

Films directed by Feng Xiaogang

Gone Forever with My Love (*Yong shi wo ai*) 1994
Yi di ji mao (TV series) 1995
The Dream Factory (*Jiafang yifang*) 1997
Be There or Be Square (*Bu jian bu san*) 1998
Sorry Baby (*Mei wan mei liao*)1999
A Sigh (*Yi sheng tan xi*) 2000
Big Shot's Funeral (*Da wan*) 2001
Cell Phone (*Shou ji*) 2003
A World Without Thieves (*Tianxia wu zei*) 2004
The Banquet (*Ye yan*) 2006
Assembly (*Ji jie hao*) 2007

Films Directed by Ning Hao

Thursday, Wednesday (*Xingqisi, Xingqisan*), 2001
Mongolian Ping Pong (*Lü caodi*) 2005
Crazy Stone (*Fengkuang de shitou*) 2006
Silver Medalist (*Yinpai cheshou*) 2008

Recuperating Displacement: the Search for Alternative Narratives in Tsai Ming-Liang's *The Hole* and *What Time is it There?*

E. K. Tan

Born in Malaysia and having attended college in Taiwan, Tsai Ming-liang is known as one of the internationally-acclaimed directors of the Second New Wave Cinema. Tsai's directorial career begins with a rather conventional debut, *Rebel of a Neon God* (1992). After the minimal success of this film, Tsai moved on to make seven others, which project denser and more abstract visions of the world as he comprehends it. These are *Vive L'amour* (1994), *The River* (1997), *The Hole* (1997), *What Time is it There?* (2001), *Goodbye Dragon Inn* (2003), *The Wayward Cloud* (2005), *I Don't Want to Sleep Alone* (2006) and his latest film at the time of writing, *Face* (2009).

Most of his films deal with the theme of time and space, in which space is always portrayed as distance between human beings, both physical and spiritual. Evolving from Tsai's obsession with depicting time and space are themes such as loneliness, isolation, melancholia, displacement, and nostalgia. This essay discusses how Tsai explores the displacement experienced by (post)modern subjects, prompting the search for alternative narratives in mass media, such as the cinema, to counter the anxieties set forth by shifting global relations, and relocating the desire to re-establish the fundamental experience of human relations.

As a trademark, Tsai usually begins his films with an 'uncanny' opening shot (something that is familiar and foreign at the same time). This shot often suggests a certain familiarity, yet embodies a sense of disorientation in form and representation. In a sense, it functions as a visual and aural trigger to arouse the curiosity of the audience. In an attempt to rearrange the fragmented content and form in relation to later events and scenes, the audience witnesses the delirious atmosphere in the opening shot mature in content and form to support the film narrative.

The Empty Space of Where Things Begin

The Hole is Tsai's fourth film. Set in an apartment building in Taipei during the week before the millennium, the film depicts two individuals' attempt to connect in their apartment building while dealing with the outbreak of the 'Taiwan Virus', an epidemic that is being spread by cockroaches. People who have contracted the virus display symptoms of 'flu and develop buglike behaviour such as crawling and photophobia. The two protagonists are known only as 'The Man Upstairs' and 'The Woman Downstairs'. Most of the residents have been evacuated since the virus has infected the building where the two reside. Those who refused to leave their apartment are quarantined and the government has issued a warning to shut down the water supply on the day of the millennium.

A plumber comes one day and leaves a hole in the living room of the Man Upstairs, creating a physical connection between him and the Woman Downstairs. However, neither one of them seizes the opportunity to communicate in the evacuated building, paralysed by the perpetual rain. Instead, it is the surrealist musical numbers in the film that reveal the desire of the Woman Downstairs to connect with the Man Upstairs. She is extremely flirtatious in her fantasy, singing and dancing in various venues of the dilapidated building with and for the Man Upstairs. Through Tsai's filmic collage of human solitude, desire and haplessness, *The Hole* emphasises the relation between collective and individual experience, in a world where humanity is at stake and the development of a narrative is impaired.

Tsai's narrative in *The Hole* is disorienting for the audience and the protagonist. One can argue that the narrative and its significance are displaced within the body of the film. Hence, the audience is led to believe that the disinterested narrative structure suggests the need to find means and substance to fill in the gap symbolised by the hole.

The film begins with an off-screen television interview with the Taiwanese people on their views of the 'Taiwan virus' and the government's measures to deal with the problem of garbage disposal that is hindering the attempt to contain the virus. A dark background and the calligraphic title of the film compose this opening shot. Mary Ann Doane defines voice-over as a technique used to transmit information through a voice that is not linked to an onscreen body. She claims that 'it is precisely because the voice is not localizable, because it cannot be yoked to a body, that it is capable of interpreting the image, producing its truth' (1986: 341). Even though Doane's essay addresses conventional voice-over commentary, it can be employed to shed light on the opening shot in the opening of *The Hole*. The voice-over supplies viewers with information related to the background of the film through the voice of authority, the TV news announcing government measures to exterminate the Taiwan Virus. Though the onscreen body represented by the Chinese character 洞 – the hole – is not linked to the voice-over in content, its presence contradicts the information transmitted by the voice-over as it literally means emptiness or hollowness, the opposite of hope as suggested by the TV news. This split in meaning between voice and image implies from the beginning that the film does not occupy a homogeneous narrative space. If the authoritative voice-over, pertaining to the truth and information of the Taiwan Virus is part of the narrative, the details are clearly displaced from the body of the film, as the film embarks on a journey to depict the haplessness and frustration suffered by the two protagonists. Instead of the actual documentary tone set off by the opening scene, the audience is introduced to a very different narrative. In a subsequent scene, while the Woman Downstairs engages in activities such as eating instant noodles and doing an egg facial, a news report regarding the Taiwan Virus appears aurally from the TV, again as voice-off. The significance of the voice-over is that it provides clinical information on the epidemic.

Nevertheless, the voice-over again exemplifies a split between the image and the voice. The audience never sees the source of the voice even when the TV that embodies the voice is a part of the shot's *mise-en-scène*.

This split between image and sound leads the audience to question the narrative structure of the film. What does Tsai's lack of interest in conventional storytelling in *The Hole* imply? The film contains no knowledge of the origin or identity of the protagonists and the building in which they reside. The two protagonists, trapped in a dilapidated building with no physical contact with the outside world, are both nameless. They live in solitude, and apart from that there is a sense of negative inertia in initiating any physical interaction between them. Even the very possibility of creating a beginning or meaning for themselves and the audience is hindered by the lack of communication. Hence, the narrative is displaced by their solitude and is further displaced by the indifferent details such as the news and the surreal musical numbers performed by the two protagonists. Linda Williams (2000) explains fantasies as myths of origins that have to do with the struggle between an irreversible fundamental experience that has actually taken place, and that of an imaginary recovery that is the link to the nostalgia for the lost object. In this sense, the fantastical musical numbers serving as fillers for the disinterested narrative in Tsai's film are more than mere fantasy. The surreal and almost irrelevant musical numbers are sublimated and displaced forms of 'a wish' or a desire belonging to the film. They constitute the basic elements for the reconciliation of the displaced wish/desire and the fundamental experience. This displaced wish/desire is one that involves the desire to restore the fundamental experience of sociality.

This wish is revealed in the central theme of the musicals in the film. The central theme that unites the five musical scenes is one of love, a basic characteristic of humanity. The first musical performance, 'Oh Calypso', is about self-love. The Woman Downstairs sings about how she can be as carefree and happy as a proud rooster. The second, 'Tiger Lady', is about marital love. She suggests in the song that her husband should leave the marriage and stop calling her Tiger Lady. 'I Want Your Love', the third musical performance, is about her desire for love. She asks for immediate attention from the Man Upstairs in response to her expression of love. In the musical number 'Achoo Cha Cha' several admirers trouble her. Finally, the film ends with 'I Don't Care Who You Are', a surreal love consummation between her and the Man Upstairs after he rescues her from her apartment through the hole. The mutual desire to connect with each other evolves with the last musical performance, merging fantasy and reality.

The musical numbers re-enact a situation that is the exact reverse of what is happening in the real-life situation for the Woman Downstairs. In actuality, she experiences a change similar to that of Gregor Samsa, Franz Kafka's protagonist in his novella *Metamorphosis*; she degenerates into a cockroach. In her fantasy, she undergoes an evolution from a proud rooster to a furious tigress to, eventually, a human being who appreciates a love that is not fixated on an object. Thus, the musical numbers substitute a condensed and transferred desire that is a link to the wish for a return to the origin of love and humanity.

A closer look at the lyrics from the last musical performance offers a clearer view of this wish.

I don't care who you are
But in your arms I cling
Alone together in the dark
Come the days of carefree spring
Swallows twirling in the blue skies
Mandarin ducks in the quiet pond
Tell me, oh tell me why, I do not know
Why do they never part?

'I don't care who you are' implies that the wish or desire is displaced from the very beginning. It is also one that cannot be fully fulfilled. Metaphorically, the fifth and sixth lines of this lyric reflect this transference of desire. Instead of the Woman Downstairs herself functioning as the subject, the 'swallows' and 'mandarin ducks' become the embodiment of love, an emotional state she wishes for but cannot have. As the last two lines, 'Tell me, oh tell me why, I do not know/Why do they never part?', imply, the subject's desire for love will always be unattainable. Like any sad ending in a movie, this claim of love as unattainable is precisely a motivating force to proffer and sustain the wish.

Since the musical numbers represent an unattainable desire, they imply the lack of links to explicit meanings in the film narrative. Interestingly, precisely because of the lack of links to meanings visible to the audience in the musical numbers, the musical fantasy in *The Hole* seduces its audience to evaluate the possible hidden meanings in the film. The fantasy sequences appear extremely awkward in the film, in contrast to the pervasive hapless, dark and desolate atmosphere of the other elements; however, it sticks out so visibly with its glamour and festive tone, which immediately makes one wonder what its function is. This awkward filling up of the narrative hole triggers the task to search for meanings hidden, and to eventually fill in the hole with a logical interpretation.

Returning to the discussion of the disinterested narrative in *The Hole*, it is the musical that is disguising the subject's desire. Hence, when we attempt to look awry at the film, the musical denatures the meaning of reality, creating, as it were, a hole in the wholeness of the film, and as a result the subject's desire surfaces. In simple terms, the musical, a different filmic style in contrast to classic narrative cinema, is adopted to replace conventional narrative. So, when the musical is removed, the subject's desire for a coherent narrative evolves.

What then is the relationship between the hole and the musical numbers? If these are ruptures to the film narrative, they nevertheless create the hole. If Tsai does not believe in the homogeneity and linearity of narrative, a rupture in his film narrative is necessary; a political gesture in transgressing the narrative form in classical cinema. The choice of a classical narrative form, the musical genre in this case, accomplishes two tasks: first, to show the arbitrariness of genre conventions; second, to incorporate the meaning of wish-fulfillment in the musical genre to uncover a wish and desire that has been suppressed by conventions. Hence, narrative in *The Hole* for Tsai is similar to the act of emptying one's own body literally (such as the purging seen in bulimics) or metaphorically (seen in meditation). It is in this very act that creates a void for a new beginning. The radio and TV voice-over in *The Hole* are made peripheral to the non-linear narrative of the film. Though cast ceaselessly outside of the body, it frames and illuminates the significance of the film that is enhanced by the musical numbers; this narrative-like voice-over frees the void for the search of a denaturalised narrative, which is less invested in plot development.

The two protagonists in *The Hole* are material metaphors of the film's struggle with narrative construction. They have bodies that are eagerly excreting substances. For example, the Man Upstairs throws up into the hole, pees in the toilet and the sink, and cries haplessly before rescuing the Woman Downstairs. They are also seen cleansing themselves by drinking water; the Man Upstairs gives the Woman Downstairs a glass of water before rescuing her, as if cleansing her of her bug-like behaviour. These bodies need to be emptied before a real connection between the two can be made possible at the end of the film. Also, it is only by emptying the interior content that desire in the body can surface. Similarly, the epidemic-affected building has to be excavated before the two protagonists can establish human attachment. Thus, the film is not really interested in emptiness but what meanings can one devise and derive at by challenging narrative conventions. Hence, the different types and levels of displacement in the film suggest that conventions isolate the individual from the fundamental experience of human connection. By challenging the linearity of narrative, the film casts conventions aside in order to illuminate the desire to connect with another human in both the Man Upstairs and the Woman Downstairs.

Time, the Marker of Existence and Displacement

In 2001 Tsai released his fifth feature film, *What Time is it There?* Adopting a similar structure to *The Hole* but engaging in a slightly more conventional narrative, the film questions and (de)constructs the meaning of time and space in a world mapped out by globalisation. Anachronism is one major theme in the film; through Xiao Kang, the male protagonist, Tsai presents a human attempt to alter the modern sense of time. The film suggests that Time as a construct is not always a cohesive force but a marker of physical separation; our notion of time connects us to the world while it simultaneously disconnects and displaces us from it. Can we escape Time by simply rejecting the common notion of time? The film seemingly suggests the impossibility of escaping time. Even if we reject the concept of time, the reality of its epistemological structure persists to haunt our everyday existence. No matter how Xiao changes clocks and watches to Paris time, the attempt still leaves him with a strong sense of helpless solitude and insipidness in the urban world. *What Time is it There?* reveals Tsai's desire to defy and define time through his protagonist; Xiao embodies the mischief in Tsai to meddle with the different ways time is conceptualised. The mischievous defiance leads to Xiao's realisation that he is stranded in a world that is responsible for his solitude; however, the transgression of time as a fixed and irrefutable concept also leads to the acknowledgment of time as circular, reversible, instead of linear. It is precisely the space beyond life and death, here and there that Xiao's relationships are mapped out in the film.

Xiao develops a fear of darkness and the ghost of his father after his father's death. He locks himself in his bedroom, sleeps with the lights on and pees in a water bottle at night. During the day, he sells counterfeit watches on the bridge outside the Taipei train station. Xiangqi, a woman getting ready for her trip to Paris, stops by one day to buy a watch. She insists on buying the watch Xiao owns personally even when he warns her about the superstition of acquiring bad luck by inheriting a possession from the relative of a recently dead person. This chance encounter between Xiao and Xiangqi makes him wonder what her trip in Paris would be like. Out of curiosity and mischief, he calls the phone company for the time in Paris and starts changing the time on his watches, the clock at home and even clocks in public venues. When his superstitious mother realises the time on the home clock has slowed down by seven hours, she stubbornly believes that her husband's ghost has returned. Hence, the family begins to accommodate the time of the ghost. In Paris, Xiangqi takes a nap in the park while some adolescents throw her luggage into the pond. A figure that resembles Xiao's father picks up the luggage for her with his umbrella.

The theme of time difference encroaches on the atmosphere of *What Time is it There?*. The film proposes at least three different ways to discuss time. First, with the death of Xiao's father, time is defined by the relationship between the living and the dead. Secondly, with Xiao's viewing of Truffaut's *Les quatre cents coups* (*The 400 Blows*) (1959),[1] time is depicted by

---

1   In this debut of Truffaut, Antoine Doinel (Jean-Pierre Léaud), a 13-year-old boy, is first seen yelled at by his parents and later bribed by them for his love and his promises to work harder in school. Soon after being pinpointed by his teacher as the class clown, Antoine ends up running away from home and his complicated family. The life of a street rat that depends on petty crimes for survival is tough yet carefree as compared to having to deal with his inattentive parents and harsh teacher.

the distinction between the past and the present. Lastly, time is marked by the physical distance between the geographical locales of Taipei and Paris.

In the scene where Xiao's mother explains to him the concept of the time of the dead, she claims that the time of the dead is slower because the dead are not as occupied as the living. The clock that has slowed down seven hours changing from Taipei time to Paris time ironically proves this. Yet the audience knows that the time change is, after all, Xiao's act of mischief. However, his mother is not wrong in claiming the new time, Paris time, belongs to the dead, as the figure of Xiao's father-lookalike returns to the living world to help pick up Xiangqi's luggage out of the pond in a different time zone, Paris time. The old man in Paris could possibly be someone who resembles the father but the enigmatic ending makes different interpretations possible.

The making of *What Time is it There?*, according to Tsai (2002) in his book of the same title, is largely influenced by the death of the father of his lead actor, Lee Kangsheng. Due to his close relationship with Lee's family, Tsai experienced the same bereavement and mourning as the family, and therefore came to understand the separation between life and death as, according to film critic Tony Rayns, 'the splitting of the action between two continents' (2002: 57). Thus, the time difference between the dead and the living becomes one main theme that connects the film. What Tsai tries to examine in this film is not only time as a presence but also time as a subject matter, a character.

Time as a character in *What Time is it There?* on the one hand generates the film's narrative and, on the other, ruptures the coherence in the daily routine of the two protagonists, Xiao and his mother. A gap is created between the modern sense of time and the significance of representational presence of a time concept within the narrative. In a sense, time depicted in the film resembles the hole in Tsai's film *The Hole*. Instead of a spatial substitute, time is a temporal substitute that is in place of some hidden meanings.

What Time is it There? begins with a series of mundane activities in the life of Xiao's father as the opening shot. The old man wakes up from a nap to switch off the rice-cooker, which is sounding off with a rhythmic beeping sound. He walks pass Xiao's room and does not see him. He ends up eating lunch alone while a fly irritates him.

Even though 'now movements'[2] relate to daily routines in relation to linear time, they do not fully describe the repetitive characteristics of the concept defined by rituals. The focus on daily routine in *What Time is it There?* extends to depict time as a product created and regulated by tradition and religious rituals in Chinese culture. In the first place, the film is centred on the death of Xiao's father and spans over the religious or superstitious belief that seven times seven weeks, which is 49 days after the death of someone, the soul will return for a last visit to the human world before it resides in the other world thereafter. According to Arthur Waley's *The Analects of Confucius*, the mourner has to lead a life apart, wear special clothes, eat special food, abstain from physical pleasures, retire from public life, and so forth (1989: 60–1). The reason for doing so is that his or her encounter with death has contaminated him; he or she is now an unclean person who needs to be segregated in order to undergo the cleansing process. This, in *What Time is it There?*, is exemplified by the mother's attempt to change everything in the house to accommodate customs and rituals relating to the dead. Being too obsessed with the rituals, she forces Xiao to join her in changing their routine to suit that of her dead husband. In an interview with film critic Danièle Rivière, Tsai confirms his beliefs in the influence of daily routine on our conception of time as he says, 'Life today makes time shorter and more rushed than before. But lots of things have changed as well around this notion of time. Different ways of life also change our notion of time, or actually change time itself' (Joyard *et al.* 1999: 105).

The concept of time in Chinese culture is marked by the practice of rituals and the concept of the everydayness of being. Life and death in this sense are extremely significant because they are the markers of one's time on earth. Also, death is not always the end of everything since the soul is promised another life in the other world (see Waley 1989). Hence, death not only defines time in the human world, it also separates and suggests a different time zone in a world that is beyond our understanding.

---

2   Heidegger discusses time as a human construct in his reading of the Aristotelian notion of time. He explains: '[The] common understanding of time comprehends only the time that reveals itself in counting as a succession of nows. From this understanding of time there arises the concept of time as a sequence of nows, which has been more particularly defined as a unidirectional irreversible sequence of nows one after the other' (1985: 141).

Besides exploring the cultural-specific conception of time marked by the distinction between the living and the dead, *What Time is it There?* also problematises the modern concept of time by highlighting the disorienting and neurotic experience suffered by Xiao who is obsessed with the presence of a different time zone, Paris. The modern concept of time is defined by the distinction between the past and the present. The present lies in the presentation of *What Time is it There?* while the past reveals itself through an intertext, which is *The 400 Blows*, a landmark of French cinema by François Truffaut.

Xiao's interest in *The 400 Blows* is inspired by his encounter with Xiangqi, the young lady who has left for Paris after buying his watch. Xiao endeavors to know, through the French film, something about Paris, which is in a different time zone introduced by Xiangqi. A specific link between Antoine, the protagonist from *The 400 Blows*, and Xiao can be identified. Like Antoine, Xiao desires to abscond from the present time and space, in which he is haunted by loneliness and the death of his father. Particularly for an audience who knows *The 400 Blows*, Xiao's desire is seen through Antoine's experience. Tsai borrows three segments from *The 400 Blows* in his film: the first clip briefly shows the Eiffel Tower; the second shows Antoine at a carnival; and finally, in the last clip, Antoine steals and drinks a huge bottle of milk. The latter two clips are very significant. Antoine is having fun in a turning cylinder in the second clip set at a carnival. As the speed of the cylinder increases, his feet are swung up from the ground. Xiao, like Antoine feels totally out of place in the life situation he is in. For Antoine, things keep happening but nothing changes. There is a need to revolt, a need to remove oneself from reality in order to reground oneself in another reality. On the other hand, although roaming the streets and engaging in petty crimes is tough and unpleasant, Antoine seems to acquire a great amount of gratification from his acts. Milk satisfies Antoine's hunger; the act of stealing satisfies his sense of individual existence. In a playful way, Tsai transforms *The 400 Blows* into an awkward detail that sticks out in the space of time to complement Xiao's wish to escape from the real world. Yet only the audience knows the parallel; once the audience identifies this, the past and present begin to function as two non-linear presences, even though the films represent the portrayal of the past and the present distinctively from two very different time settings. Xiao mingles with Antoine from the past in his room via a TV screen; while the now middle-aged Jean-Pièrre Léaud, who was Antoine in *The 400 Blows* appears in the Luxembourg garden talking and giving Xiangqi his phone number. Also, like Antoine with his delinquent pranks, Xiao goes around changing the time on clocks in public places.

The time difference between Taipei and Paris is highlighted by Xiao's encounter with Xiangqi while the journey to comprehend time is triggered by the seemingly unbefitting *The 400 Blows*. We are trained to rationalise time and its different manifestations according to a predetermined structure without knowing or questioning the epistemological construction behind it. Time, as a character in the film, intrudes into Xiao's life by disorienting his ontological experience. The intrusion prompts Xiao to want to resolve or make sense of the alienating experience that ruptures his understanding of daily routine. In a sense, time here performs the same function as the hole in *The Hole* in suggesting a displacement of meanings in the film narrative.

What makes *What Time is it There?* different from *The Hole* is the circular ending. Time is reversible with the proposal of a possible reincarnation marked by the return of the father in the final scene. Tony Rayns analyses the ending as harbouring

> the possibility that reincarnation may be (a) literally true, (b) poetically credible, or (c) a valid metaphor for the process of coming to terms with bereavement. By design, the film ends with a symmetrical shot of a perfect circle – actually the millennium Ferris wheel by the Tuileries – connoting both narrative closure and the wished-for fantasy of cyclical return. (2002: 57)

The wish fulfillment suggested by Rayns is not necessarily that of the characters since Xiao's mother does not know that 'her husband' will end up in a different time zone and is actually separated by water, a vision she sees earlier on, aided by the Taoist priest; Xiao does not know that a more direct connection between Paris, Xiangqi and himself is facilitated by 'his father's' presence in Paris. However, the audience knows. It is a wish fulfillment for the audience to see their wishes fulfilled, as the ending presents to some extent a happy ending. It is also a wish fulfillment for Tsai, as he unpacks a series of personal concerns relating to life and death, the question of mortality, and the significance of traditions through the symbol of the dead father and Truffaut's *The 400 Blows*.

Underneath the depiction of the two time concepts is a fundamental experience waiting to be identified by the audience by activating the alienated desire. First, Xiao's father, with his death, denatures the film narrative and challenges the modern concept of time by suggesting an alternative way of conceptualising time, the time of the dead. Second, *The 400 Blows* troubles Xiao with a different time conception, alternatively functioning as transference for his desire to escape time. The circular ending of *What Time is it There?* suggests the irreversibility of time with the metaphorical return of the dead father in Paris. It is in this return that the displacement in time and experience has been reckoned for the audience who witnesses Xiao's alienation and isolation as an effect of time displacement.

This scene in Paris does not necessary provide a closure to the film since it ends with Xiao returning home and reconciling with his mother by lying next to her in bed. What is interesting is that the narrative actually further closes with two moments that comes after the film is complete: the train station overhead bridge in Taipei, where Xiao vends his watches, is torn down; the millennium Ferris wheel by the Tuileries is also removed. Temporality is made permanent, to a certain extent through technology in Tsai's work; time is reversible with human intervention to (re)create meanings out of the split in time marked by physical and material existence.

Time, the ultimate Time, is not accessible to us humans as we are all living in Time. In order to better the knowledge of ourselves, we utilise language to state our state of being. Hence the concept of time is created to aid our control over the temporality of our actions; categories are laid out – Past, Present and Future. By laying out the several sets of time difference in *What Time is it There?*, Tsai highlights the gaps and crevices in our development of the concept of time. It is precisely in these gaps and crevices that different kinds of connections between individuals are established.

Conclusion

Spatial and temporal displacement are the two main forms of alienating experience depicted in *The Hole* and *What Time is it There?*. The main protagonists in both films come to learn that their existence falls out of place from the urbanisation of social relations due to global flows that emphasise economic and technological growth. Though displaced and constantly negotiating with the environment they are stranded in, the protagonists are not free from the existential question of life and death, and the increasing threat of viruses and disease. Unlike themes of haplessness and isolation, which are often discussed and emphasised as the sole experiences in Tsai's work, the glimpses of hope in his narratives are often neglected. The physical hole in the apartments of the protagonists of *The Hole*, and the time gaps between different temporal structures of Time, are metaphors of the alienation between (post)modern individuals. Tsai sensitively manipulates these gaps and crevices as structural rupture to conventional storytelling in fictional films in order to construct alternative narratives to restore the displace connections in human relationships. The space, be it physical in *The Hole* or imaginary in *What Time is it There?*, is transformed from a product of displacement to a facilitator to the recuperation of estranged human relationships. Tsai Ming-liang is not a director who imagines that his works purport the truth to our existence; he explores different possibilities to conceptualise the self and its relationship with the world with us.

Bibliography

Doane, Mary Ann (1986) 'The Voice in the Cinema: The Articulation of Body and Space', in Philip Rosen (ed.) *Narrative, Apparatus, Ideology: A Film Theory Reader*. New York: Columbia University Press, 335–48.

Heidegger, Martin (1985) *History of the Concept of Time*, Trans. Theodore Kisiel. Indiana: Indiana University Press.

Joyard, Olivier, Jean-Pierre Rehm and Daniele Rivière (1999) *Tsai Ming-liang*. Trans. J. Ames Hodges and Andrew Rothwell. Paris: Dis Voir.

Rayns, Tony (2002) '*What time is it there?*', *Sight and Sound*, July, 57.

Tsai, Ming-liang (2002) *What Time is it There?* Taipei: Aquarius.

Waley, Arthur (1989) *The Analects of Confucius*. New York: Vintage Books.

Williams, Linda (2000) 'Film Bodies: Gender, Genre, and Excess', in Toby Miller and Robert Stam (eds) *Film and Theory: An Anthology*. Cambridge, MA: Blackwell, 207–22.

De-Mystifying a Postwar Myth: Reading Fukasaku's *Jinginaki Tatakai*

Masashi Ichiki

When it was released in January 1973, *Jinginaki Tatakai* (a.k.a *Battle without Honour and Humanity*) was not expected to be a hit. It was originally designed as a 60-minute, mono-colour programmer expected to fill out the minor part of Toei's double bills (see Yamane & Nonehara 2005). However, this quite violent and chaotic movie based upon a memoir of a Hiroshima *yakuza* boss (written in a prison cell) turned out to be a studio-saving hit for Toei and a career milestone for Fukasaku Kinji. In four movie theatres in downtown Tokyo (called *Ichiban-kan*, the top-rank theatres, under the program picture system), *Jinginaki Tatakai* attracted more than 150,000 viewers in the first three weeks, which exceeded the previous film in the same theatres by 5 to 40 per cent (see Kasahara 2005).[1] Within the same year, Toei produced two more instalments of the series. All of them were commercially successful and Toei's income rose from 6.2 billion yen in 1972 to 7.3 billion yen in 1973.[2] In short, *Jinginaki Tatakai* served as the beachhead for Toei to compete with television in the years when the popularity of Japanese cinema was in a significant decline. Yet despite all its popular appeal, film critics have generally been indifferent to this mega-hit series. Unlike

---

1   *Showa Zankyo-den: Yabure-gasa* (*The Last Chivalry: A Broken Umbrella*) (1973), directed by Saeju Kiyoshi, written by Murao Akira and starring Ken Takakura and Ando Noburu.
2   The respective movie-going figures are based on tables in *Kinema Jumpo*, vol. 598, p. 91 and vol. 624, p. 95.

more artistic or more socially conscious films by Oshima Nagisa, Imamura Shohei and Kurosawa Akira, *Jinginaki Tatakai* sequels (and by the same token, Toei's *yakuza* films as a whole) have been considered 'low culture' films which were produced for entertainment's sake only and thus do not deserve critical attention. The general indifference of film critics toward *Jinginaki Tatakai* can at least partially be explained by the fact that the film's sequels were produced, distributed and consumed within the program picture system. Under this mass-production/mass-distribution system, Japanese movie companies produced a large number of films and distributed them weekly. In its heyday, in 1963, Toei produced 103 movies a year and in 1973, the year it produced *Jinginaki Tatakai*, Toei produced 55 movies, though the number of filmgoers had dropped to 200 million, 80 per cent less than the peak year. Accordingly, each film was produced with a limited budget and in a very short production period. In the case of *Jinginaki Tatakai*, Kasahara Kazuo had 69 days to complete the script (Kasahara 1998) and Fukasaku filmed it in just 25 days (Fukasaku & Yamane 2003). The prior set opening date resulted in no possibility of overrunning the production schedule.

Though it is true that 'masterpieces of Japanese films are produced under the program picture system' (Watanabe 2008: 3), it is also true that a large number of films produced under such conditions are often of poor quality and often of a highly generic nature. The *Jinginaki Tatakai* sequels serve as a good example again. When the series came to an end with the fifth instalment, *Kanketsu-hen* (*The Final Episode*), Toei refused to let a profitable franchise die and decided to produce a four-volume series titled *Shin Jinginaki Tatakai* (*New Battles without Honour*). Though the new series was also directed by Fukasaku and starred Sugawara Bunta, it was based on a highly fictionalised original story and characters. The *Shin Jinginaki Tatakai* series was followed by *Sonogono Jinginaki Tatakai* (*The Battles without Honour: Afterwards*), which was a completely different story featuring a new director, new plots and new characters. *Sonogono Jinginaki Tatakai* and the original series share nothing in common except the title. In short, under the program picture system, being a profitable entertainment is all that matters; filmmakers have to follow the given formula of *yakuza* films, that is, known plots, recognisable and familiar characters and obvious iconography (see McDonald 1992) and there is little room for auteurism, or the reflection of filmmakers' personal creative vision.

Yet there are two factors which lead us to re-evaluate what has been considered 'low culture' and thus does not deserve critical attention. First, creators of the films, most notably director Fukasaku and scriptwriter Kasahara, seem to be determined to integrate their ideas about post-war Japan into this entertainment series. A closer look at the film reveals that micro-narratives of Hiroshima gang wars depicted in *Jinginaki Tatakai* are often contained within the meta-narratives of Japan's post-war history (see Sato 1974; Nishitani 2007). At the same time, Tessa Morris Suzuki's discussion offers an interesting point of view; in *The Past Within Us* (2005), she emphasises the significance of popular media in the process through which history is passed on and suggests that films, with their audio-visual impact, presents a single narrative on historical events, which results in the emergence of a communal memory. Suzuki states: 'The movie, meanwhile, creates a single, unforgettable, widely influential narrative. Like the legends of oral societies, it embodies a moral and narrative structure which shapes popular images of the world in which we live. The movie provides modern society with its mythology' (2005: 147). Suzuki's discussion helps us to shed different light on *Jinginaki Tatakai*. Again, it was one of the most popular films in the history of Japanese cinema, and it is estimated that not only has the series attracted more than 9 million filmgoers in total, but its VHS/DVD sales are close to 400,000 units. These figures are quite significant in that they attest to the size of 'the remembering community' (Suzuki 2005: 156) that *Jinginaki Tatakai* has established. In other words, the fact that the images of modern Japan presented in this mega-hit film are shared by a large number of viewers and thus affects their perception cannot be dismissed. Drawing upon this understanding, let us begin our discussion by examining the representations of A-bomb survivors in *Jinginaki Tatakai*. In so doing, I hope to illustrate that presentation of this constituency offers an important insight into understanding Fukasaku's ideas on post-war Japan.

A-bomb Slum: An Unchanged Place in a Changing Landscape

In the *Jinginaki Tatakai* series, we sometimes come across a long shot of small, dilapidated shacks crowded together on a riverbank. One glance at the shot tells the viewer that it is the landscape of a slum. In discussing the representations of A-bomb survivors in *Jinginaki Tatakai*, this is a good place to start, for the shots are always accompanied by a caption which says 'Motomachi, Hiroshima, aka, A-bomb slum.' Let us take a look at Fumisawa Ryuichi's explanation of the A-bomb slum:

> At the heart of Hiroshima lies a huge vacant area. This is Motomachi. Called Aioi-dori, this area is considered a forbidden zone created by the A-bomb. Across the street from the A-bomb Dome, a narrow and unpaved street stretches along a riverbank for about 1 kilometre. Along the street, there are about 900 shacks in which 1,135 families dwell. (1965: 2)

As Fumisawa's term, 'a forbidden zone created by the A-bomb' implies, Motomachi is a section of Hiroshima where, unable to find other places to live in, A-bomb survivors were confined. We first come across the A-bomb slum in the second instalment of the series, *Hiroshima Shito-hen* (*Hiroshima Deadly Battles*). In the film, the A-bomb slum is presented as a filthy and chaotic place; the roads are unpaved and dusty, the houses are messy and shabby, and confusion fills the air. Furthermore, the disorderly atmosphere makes it a convenient hideout for criminals. Ohtomo, one of the gang bosses, hides in the A-bomb slum, trying to dodge police as well as his rival gang. A clue to understanding the significance of the A-bomb slum in *Hiroshima Shito-hen* lies in the criticism of the film. The film was often criticised for fictionalising actual events, though Toei advertised it as a '*Jitsuroku* (Docu-drama)' film, a realistic description of the actual events. The most notable modification is in the time frame; while the actual events occurred between 1946 and 1948, the film changes the time frame to the period between 1946 and 1955. This alteration is mandated by Toei for economic reasons; Kasahara (1998) recalls that Toei requested the modification to cut the substantial cost of making a new film set. At the same time, as a concomitant effect of this modification, *Hiroshima Shito-hen* comes to show the changing landscape of Hiroshima. The first part of the film is set in 1946 and we see Hiroshima reduced to rubble by the atomic blast. In the sequence of Yamanaka's lynching in a marketplace at the onset of the film, the roads are unpaved and narrow, the houses are small and shabby, and there are still ruins here and there. Confusion dominates the street and, without any police in sight, no one can stop the brutal lynching that we see take place. In the latter part, set approximately a decade later in 1955, Hiroshima's landscape has drastically been changed. In the final sequence in which Yamanaka commits suicide, we see rows of decent, modern houses along the clean, neatly paved street. The streets are filled with police and patrol car sirens, which indicate that law and order has been established. In short, as it depicts Hiroshima over a ten-year period, the second instalment presents the transformation of Hiroshima, from ruins to a city with a modern landscape.

The underlying theme of changing landscape in *Hiroshima Shito-hen* is strengthened by Fukasaku's cinematic elaborations. First, Fukasaku alters Kasahara's original script so that the theme becomes even clearer. A scene in which a police chief confronts Muraoka, a Hiroshima *yakuza* boss, is a case in point. Irritated by the rude manner of the police chief, Muraoka angrily reminds the police chief that he had begged Muraoka for help ten years before. In Kasahara's script, the police chief responds to Muraoka by saying 'Mr Muraoka, we have our priorities' (Kasahara 1998: 159). In the scene filmed by Fukasaku, the police chief tells Muraoka 'time has changed and we are not what we were', as he blows cigarette smoke into Muraoka's face. Here, with the elaboration by Fukasaku, the shift of power between the police and *yakuza* is made even clearer. Though they were once powerless and needed the *yakuzas'* help in establishing law and order, the police now stand tall and dismiss them as a viable political and social power.

In addition, Fukasaku employs another cinematic technique to dramatically illustrate how much the landscape of Hiroshima has changed in the years depicted in the movie. It has been claimed (Fukasaku & Yamane 2003; Nomura 2003) that the second instalment is the only one in the series that Fukasaku filmed on location in Hiroshima and used actual scenes of the city. Thus, what is actually contrasted in the film are both the images of Hiroshima amidst the confusion of the immediate post-war period *and* those of the 1970s, more than twenty years after the war when the city was completely reconstructed. With such deliberation, the contrast between the two becomes more vivid, thereby making the theme of a changing landscape come more prominently to the fore. When we take into account this underlying theme of *Hiroshima Shito-hen*, we are able to examine what lies behind Fukasaku's presentation of the A-bomb slum. The scenery of the slum of 1955 is surprisingly similar to that of Hiroshima right after the war. In other words, realising how much the landscape of Hiroshima has changed is equivalent to realising how intact the landscape of the A-bomb slum has remained. In the long shot of the slum in *Hiroshima Shito-hen*, we can see dilapidated, half-standing houses crowded together on a river and in the distance there is a tall, white building. The contrast between the two eloquently illustrates what Fukasaku intends in his representation of the area. By showing the contrast between what has changed and what has not, Fukasaku calls attention to the fact that there are people whose lives have not altered much in a city which rapidly recovered from the devastation of war. The atomic blast killed more than ten thousand people in an instant and turned approximately seventy per cent of Hiroshima into ruins. As the term *genshi-ya* ('the Atomic field') testifies, the destruction of the city by a nuclear weapon is unprecedented in its thoroughness and intensity and, as Nakatani Ayahito (2000) suggests, Hiroshima's reconstruction refers not to rebuilding the lost city, but to reinventing a whole new city. Various measures were taken to support Hiroshima's reincarnation into a symbol of suffering and peace, and in 1949 the Diet passed the Hiroshima Peace Memorial City Law and provided financial assistance for the city's reconstruction programme, which enabled the construction of the Peace Boulevard and the Hiroshima Peace Memorial Park among others.

While the city was promptly reconstructed, assistance to and support of the A-bomb survivors was not offered as quickly. With the Occupation policy of keeping information about the A-bomb confidential and placing priority on research rather than on treating the victims, the plight of A-bomb survivors largely fell on deaf ears, and they had to struggle for survival on their own. It was not until 1956 that the A-bomb hospital, which specialised in medical treatment of survivors, was established. Additionally, it was not until 1957 that the Diet passed the A-bomb Medical Act, the first legal attempt to help the victims financially. As indicated by Nakano Kazunori (2005), the time lapse between 1949 and 1956 attests to the fact that A-bomb survivors were left unattended in a city that had undergone rapid construction. Needless to say, the wretched condition of the survivors is personified in the A-bomb slum. Having lost everything and being severely handicapped by the bomb itself, the survivors had no choice but to live in a deteriorated slum. In this sense, Fukasaku's depiction of the slum – a place that remained intact in a rapidly changing landscape – is an indictment of the maltreatment of the victims.

A *Jinginaki* Murder and the A-bomb Factor

If the slum in 1955 is the post-war confusion manifested in a reconstructed Hiroshima, then what about the slum of 1964? We revisit the slum in the fourth instalment, *Chojo Sakusen* (*The High Tactics*). In this film describing a triangular battle among the Yamamura gang, the Uchimoto gang and civil society, Fukasaku brings his camera into one of the rundown houses and shows the viewers what it was like to be an A-bomb survivor. Let us examine in detail a sequence which involves the murder of a *yakuza* named Fujita by a younger one, Nozaki, whom Fujita had acted as a patron to. On a superficial level, Nozaki murders Fujita to whom he owes *giri* (ethical obligations), because he is manipulated by his boss. Nozaki's boss wants a monopoly on the money he shares with Fujita's gang and he tells Nozaki that Nozaki could be rich without Fujita. This is a typical sequence in the *Jinginaki Tatakai* series, which is filled with conspiracies and backstabbing murders of this sort. At the same time, however, a closer look into the sequence indicates that Fukasaku deliberately constructed it so that the fact of Nozaki's being an A-bomb survivor underlies his shameless murder of Fujita. The sequence starts with a long shot of the slum; following this first shot, the camera zooms to one of the houses and then the shot switches to inside the house. Five people, Nozaki, his mother and his siblings, are crammed into a small, messy shack. Nozaki's small siblings are watching television despite that fact it is broken and they can hardly make out the broadcasted images. Nozaki's mother, who is elderly and sick, is so irritated with the noise from the broken TV that she yells at the children to turn it off. At this point, Nozaki leaves the house, saying he will buy them a brand new TV. The sequence is followed by another in which Nozaki visits Fujita late at night, points a gun at him, and kills him. In decoding this sequence, it is important to note that Fukasaku employs a number of cinematic icons, which appeal to the collective memories of the audience and manipulate their perception of the sequence. The first icon to be examined here is the broken TV in Nozaki's house. For the majority of *Jinginaki Tatakai* viewers who grew up in the 1950s and 1960s, a TV was a symbol of prosperity. The hyper-economic boom of the post-war period dramatically improved the once-devastated Japanese economy and raised the living standard of Japanese families. Television, along with the washing machine and refrigerator, symbolised this newly-achieved economic prosperity as one of the three 'Imperial regalia'. The commonly-held notion of TV as a symbol of prosperity highlights the fact that Nozaki's family, who cannot afford a new TV, has been left out of the economic prosperity of the time.

The second icon is found in the structure of a shot which captures the face of Nozaki's mother. The frame in question has two objects, Nozaki and his mother in a dark, messy house. Nozaki's face is shot in close-up, but the focus is shallow and our attention is directed to his mother in the background. Her right upper-body is shot in medium close-up. The focus is on her aged face, on which we see a large keloidal burn, a stereotypical image of A-bomb victims. This shot is reminiscent of one of the most famous images of the bombing victims, a picture taken by Yamahata Yosuke. Yamahata's picture shows the right upper-body of a young mother breastfeeding her baby. The mother and her baby are shot in medium close-up and are the only recognisable object in the frame. On the mother's white face, there is a burn of noticeable size, which implies what she has experienced. Comparing the two images, we can see that Fukasaku's shot structure is similar to that of Yamahata's in setting, in camera's angle and in shot size, in addition to the fact that both women have an identical burn on a similar part of their faces. The resemblance between the two shots indicates that Fukasaku deliberately constructed his to remind his audience of Yamahata's and to emphasise the fact that the Nozakis are A-bomb survivors, just like Yamahata's young mother.

Thus, in Nozaki's shooting of Fujita to buy his family a brand new TV, there is the implication that this is the inevitable outcome of their being survivors. By using these cinematic icons, the sequence places being an A-bomb victim, living in poverty and becoming a criminal in a direct cause/ effect relation. The sequence insists that, left out of the prosperity due to the aftereffects of the bomb, victims like Nozaki have no choice but to resort to a life of crime. Depicting survivors as marginalised beings on the verge of being a menace to society sharply contradicts the dominant images that proliferated in post-war Japan. The A-bomb survivors have largely been depicted as those who passively accepted their suffering as their fate, lived their life as fully as possible against all the odds, and died quietly when the time came. This image is by no means a reflection of who the survivors really are, but the personification of who Japanese society would wish them to be. As Tasaki Hiroaki points out (2002), the socio-political situation of the post-war period did not allow Japan to prosecute the dropping of the A-bomb as a war crime and it came to be regarded more as an unavoidable natural disaster rather than a savage act of mass murder. Thus, survivors were expected to accept their suffering with the sense of *mono-no-aware*, a sorrowful resignation which Donald Richie (1996) finds characteristic of Japanese A-bomb films.

It is important to note that expecting A-bomb survivors to bear the unbearable offers a convenient excuse for ignoring the problems that they face, for their canonisation allows Japanese society to regard the issue of these survivors not as a socio-political issue for which Japanese society is responsible but as a moral issue in which the mental strength of the survivors is tested. Perhaps Oe Kenzaburo is a good example. In his *Hiroshima Notes* (1981), Oe repeatedly writes of the people he calls 'the Moralists of Hiroshima', or the un-surrendered people. Oe finds that they are endowed with extreme mental strength and only through their inner strength can they maintain their sanity. He writes:

> Suppose a brutal murderer appears and is apprehended, and we learn that he was led to commit heinous crimes out of despair over being bombed in Hiroshima. Who on earth would have the courage to look the criminal squarely in the eye? It is simply our good fortune that we have not had such criminals appear to force the question of our own guilt. And we should acknowledge gratefully that this good fortune results from the surprising spirit of self-restraint of the Hiroshima people who had every reason to fall into such despair. (1981: 154–5)

Now it is clear that Oe's worst nightmare is personified in Nozaki of *Chojo Sakusen*. He does not have the inner strength which Oe thinks he sees in the moralists of Hiroshima, and the very fact of his being an A-bomb survivor drives him to a criminal act. In representing survivors this way, Fukasaku exposes the deception behind the canonised image of them: he unveils the fact that the A-bomb survivors are not saints that Japanese society wish and expect them to be, and that their marginalisation in post-war Japan has pushed them to the edge.

Why the Yakuza Wars in Hiroshima: Demystifying Hiroshima

The focus will now turn to the issue of the cinematic format employed for *Jinginaki Tatakai*, that is, the *Jitsuroku* format. The Hiroshima *yakuza* wars, being the longest and the bloodiest series of *yakuza* wars in modern Japan, is ideal material for *yakuza* films. Thus, Okada Shigeru, the president of Toei at the time, strongly pushed the filming project, and Toei acquired the filming rights soon after the original documentary by Iiboshi Koichi appeared in *Weekly Sankei* (see Uechi 1998; Takahashi 2003). In filming this material, Toei decided to employ a completely new cinematic format. Replacing the *Ninkyo* style of the preceding decade, which was characterised by an aesthetic depiction of the conflict between two opposing values, of *giri* and *ninjo* (humane sentiment) as well as of good and evil, Toei invented the *Jitsuroku* format, a docu-drama style which emphasised a realistic description of raw violence. Shundo Koji, a Toei's film producer who was in charge of the *yakuza* film assembly line, brought in Fukasaku to direct the film, though many in the production team opposed the idea by saying he was too 'self-centred' (see Shundo & Yamane 1999: 200). Fukasaku multiplied the bloodiness of the story by fully utilising the cinematic devices for which he was known – hand-held cameras, zoom lenses and natural lighting, among others. Hiroshima's *yakuza* wars were so violent that the filming of them required a new and more violent form of expression. Now, on a socio-historical level, why did the *yakuza* wars occur in this particular place on such a large scale and last for so long? In answering this question, we have to view Hiroshima not as a mystic symbol of tragedy and peace but in a more historical context.

Though it is true that the post-war chaos bred unlawful organisations in many parts of Japan, various accounts of the Hiroshima *yakuza* wars agree that the seeds were planted in the socio-historical background of the area (see Iiboshi 1980; Hondo 2003). Since the Meiji period, Hiroshima had developed as the military capital, housing the second General Army Headquarters, which commanded the defence of all of southern Japan. The city was a communications centre, a storage point and an assembly area for troops as well as a supply and logistics base for the Japanese military. The area's military significance was strengthened by Kure, a city only twenty kilometres away from Hiroshima. Kure had a naval arsenal, one of the largest shipbuilding plants in Asia, and served as the mother port for the Japanese Imperial Navy. In short, the Hiroshima region was the frontline base of the Imperial Japan's aggression toward Asia.

Being the military capital incited the rapid emergence of *yakuza* organisations after the war. Being military centres, the economy of the region depended greatly upon military-related industries. Thus, the end of the war had a significant effect upon the social as well as economic infrastructure of the region. With the disarmament of the Japanese military, the mainstay of the regional economy suddenly disappeared and many became unemployed. At the same time, while many suffered from a severe shortage of food, plenty of military supplies remained untouched in military depots in Hiroshima where a number of military facilities had been located. It is estimated that approximately three to four billion yen worth of supplies were kept in Hiroshima. In the chaos of the post-war period, survival was the norm of the time, and these military supplies became a target for burglary. The Occupation policy to completely disarm the civil police made it difficult to maintain order over such criminal acts. As Hondo Junichiro states, 'The end of war made Kure a city of unemployed, then, of outlaws' (2003: 73).

While being the military capital fuelled unlawful activities in Hiroshima and thus helped the emergence of *yakuza* organisations there, another military city played a significant role in maintaining the bloody *yakuza* wars for a lengthy period of time. It is Iwakuni, forty kilometres down the coast from Hiroshima, where a US marine base was established in 1950. The Iwakuni base was used as a springboard for aircrafts heading first to the Korean War, and then to the Vietnam War. In this sense, even after the end of World War II, war and aggression, which post-war Japan had declared it had renounced, continued in Iwakuni, and it is this continuation of war that affected the *yakuza* wars in Hiroshima. It has been argued that the supply of firearms was steady and plentiful in the Hiroshima underworld (see *Chugoku* 1975; Kasahara 2005), and Matsuoka Shigeru even suggests that 'the price of the handguns in Hiroshima was probably the cheapest' (1973: 119). The majority of firearms in Hiroshima are believed to have been either smuggled ones from the Iwakuni base or those from the old Imperial military. In short, behind the violent *yakuza* wars in Hiroshima lies the fact that war and aggression have always been so close.

Depicting the *yakuza* wars in docu-drama format, that is, depicting raw violence in a realistic manner, almost inevitably brings up the memory of the war and aggression, and places it at the heart of the violent scenes *Jinginaki Tatakai* presents. Fukasaku shows it in a symbolic way. As the series develops, Hirono, the protagonist of the series, changes his outfit from a GI uniform, to a loud Hawaiian shirt, then to a suit – a typical gangster outfit – which serves to indicate that the war, post-war confusion and *yakuza* violence are all interrelated.

Recontexualising Hiroshima into its socio-historical context is a highly political act in post-war Japan, in that it challenges the post-war notion of the city entirely. In post-war Japan, Hiroshima is regarded as the first victim of the nuclear era and has been made into a symbol of social discourse of victimisation. Kan Sang-jung (1995) and Yoneyama Risa (2005) both point out that the memories of war proliferated in post-war Japan are highly problematic, in that they tend to focus on the atrocity Japanese suffered towards the end of the war and to forget the atrocity Japanese forced upon Asia during hostilities. Kurihara Sadako tries to unveil the collective amnesia of post-war Japan in her '*Hiroshima-to Iu-toki*' ('When We Speak of Hiroshima'), which reads in part:

> When we speak of Hiroshima, they speak of Pearl Harbor
> When we speak of Hiroshima, they speak of the rape of Nanking
> When we speak of Hiroshima, they speak of the Manila Massacre
> In which our soldiers set fire on non-combatants,
> When we speak of Hiroshima, blood and fire echoes back. (1976: 103)

Kurihara makes it clear that Hiroshima's victimhood will not excuse it from being the major part of Imperial Japan's aggression. In short, Hiroshima has been de-historicised into a symbol of suffering and then of peace.

By presenting *yakuza* violence in a realistic way, Fukasaku re-historicises what post-war Japan has de-historicised. He indicates that the bloody *yakuza* wars in Hiroshima are the legacy of the city's involvement in war and aggression, not only in the past but also in the present. In *Kanketu-hen*, Fukasaku dramatically presents his opposition to the post-war amnesia. This fifth episode begins with a scene in which a group of *yakuzas* in black suits and sporting sunglasses, easily recognisable markers of gangsters, marches on one of Hiroshima's streets on an A-bomb Memorial Day. They carry a big banner which reads 'Eternal Peace to Japan' and a bouquet to be offered to the A-bomb victims, while all around them are riot police. We are told by voice-over narration that, in order to evade the crackdown by law enforcement, *yakuzas* in Hiroshima had formed a political organisation and stand for peace. Fukasaku never fails to expose the deceitful nature of the *yakuzas*' shift from an unlawful pack of violent gangsters to a peaceful political organisation. In the sequence which immediately follows, we see lower members of the organisation, still in black suits from the march, complaining that 'this political organisation business is just bunk'. Not only that, in the next moment, they start a fight with members of a rival gang. Fukasaku even makes Matsumura, the new boss of the *yakuza*/political organisation say that 'No matter what outfit we have, we are *yakuzas* after all.'

It is obvious that the ironic depiction of *yakuzas*' political organisation in *Kanketsu-hen* points directly toward Hiroshima's mystic status as a symbol of suffering and peace. Just as the outfits of a political organisation do not necessarily dismiss the fact that they are *yakuzas*, Hiroshima's being victimised by the A-bomb does not eradicate its past as the military capital in Imperial Japan. Through depicting the raw violence of *yakuzas* wars in Hiroshima, Fukasaku demystifies the post-war myth of Hiroshima.

Conclusion

This essay has presented a socio-cultural analysis of one of the most popular entertainment films in Japan, focusing on its representations of A-bomb victims. The A-bomb survivors are depicted not as saints, as post-war Japan wishes they were, but as members of a social underclass who are left out of post-war prosperity and whose despair, which Japanese society often tends to ignore, leaves them few options other than becoming criminals. *Jinginaki Tatakai* not only exposes the post-war myth of Hiroshima as a product of collective amnesia, but the myth also offers a convenient excuse by which to ignore the plight of survivors. Beneath the realistic description of *yakuza* violence of *Jinginaki Tatakai* lies Fukasaku's critical view on social injustice in post-war Japan. Successfully incorporating his blistering social conscience into a highly entertainment-oriented film genre, Fukasaku has made *Jinginaki Tatakai* a classic of post-war Japanese film.

Bibliography

Chugoku (1975) *Aru Yuki-no Kiroku: Kyoki-no Shita-no Shuzai Note.* Tokyo: Seishun Shuppan.

Fukasaku, Kinji and Sadao Yamane (2003) *Eiga Kantoku Fukasaku Kinji.* Tokyo: Wise Shuppan.

Fumisawa, Ryuichi (1965) 'Aioi-dori', in T. Yamashiro (ed.) *Kono Sekai-no Katasumi-de.* Tokyo: Iwanami Shoten, 1–30.

Hondo, Junichiro (2003) *Hiroshima Yakuza-den.* Tokyo: Gento-sha.

Iiboshi, Koichi (1980) *Jinginaki Tatakai: Shito-hen.* Tokyo: Kadokawa Shoten.

Kan, Sang-jung (1995) *Futatsu-no Sengo-to Nihon: Ajia-kara Tou Sengo 50nen.* Tokyo: San-ichi Shobo.

Kasahara, Kazuo (1998) *Jinginaki Tatakai: Jinginaki Tatakai, Hiroshima Shito-hen, Dairi Senso, and Chojo Saksen.* Tokyo: Gento-sha.

_____ (2005) *Jinginaki Tatakai: Tyosa-Shuzai-Roku Shusei.* Tokyo: Ohta Shuppan.

Kurihara, Sadako (1976) *Hiroshima-to Iu-toki.* Tokyo: San-ichi Shobo.

Matsuoka, Shigeru (1973) '*Jinginaki Tatakai* ni egakareta jijitu-gonin', *Eiga Hyoron,* 30, 7, 116–26.

McDonald, Keiko I. (1992) 'The Yakuza Film: An Introduction', in A. Nolletti, Jr. and D. Desser (eds) *Reframing Japanese Cinema: Authorship, Genre, History.* Bloomington: Indiana University Press, 165–92.

Nakano, Kazunori (2005) 'Shinsho fukei-to shiteno hibaku-toshi', *Journal of Genbaku Literature,* 4, 130–47.

Nakatani, Ayahito (2003) 'Basho-to-kukan: Senko keitai-ron', in K. Ueta, N. Jinno, Y. Nishimura and Y. Mamiya (eds) *Iwanami-koza: Toshi-no Saisei-wo Kangaeru*, vol. 1, 67–99.

Nishitani, Koji (2007) 'Sensoeiga-toshiteno *Jinginaki Takakaï*, *Kindai*, 98, 35–50.

Nomura, Masaaki (2003) 'Fukunaga Kuniaki Interview', in S. Hasumi, M. Matsushita, N. Nakamura and M. Nakao (eds) *Jinginaki Tatakai Perfect Book*. Tokyo: Takarajima Shuppan, 92–5.

Oe, Kenzaburo (1981) *Hiroshima Notes*. Trans. D. L. Swain and T. Yonezawa. New York: Grove Press.

Richie, Donald (1996) '*Mono-no-aware*: Hiroshima on film', in M. Broderick (ed.) *Hibakusha Cinema: Hiroshima, Nagasaki and the Nuclear Image in Japanese Film*. New York: Columbia University Press, 28–47.

Sato. Tadeo (1974) 'Fukasaku Kinji-no Sekai', in *Film Directors of the World*, in T. Uryu (ed.), 22, 55–70.

Shundo, Koji and Sadao Yamane (1999) *Ninkyo Eiga-den*. Tokyo: Kodan-sha.

Suzuki, Tessa M. (2005) *The Past Within Us: Media, Memory, History*. London: Verso.

Takahashi, Satoshi (2003) *Muho-Chitai*. Tokyo: Ohta Shuppan.

Tasaki, Hiroki (2002) 'Genbaku bungaku-no Shuhen', *Journal of Genbaku Literature*, 1, 34–57.

Uechi, Takeshi (1998) 'Interview with Goro Kusakabe', in J. Sugisaku and T. Uechi (eds) *Jinginaki Tatakai Roman Album*. Tokyo: Tokuma Shoten, 128–34.

Yamane, Sadao and Naoshi Yonehara (2005) *Jinginaki Tataki-wo Tukutta Otokotachi*. Tokyo: NHK Shuppan.

Yoneyama. Risa (2005) *Hiroshima Traces: Time, Space, and the Dialectics of Memory*. Trans. H. Ozawa *et al*. Tokyo: Iwanami Shoten.

Watanabe, Takenobu (2008) 'Program Picture-towa nanika', *Mirai*, 496, 1–6.

Gathering Dust in the Wind: Memory and the 'Real' in Rithy Panh's *S21*

Saër Maty Bâ

> 'I have now spent half of my life in France … but I was born in Cambodia and have French citizenship … I am francophone.'
>
> Rithy Panh (in Blum-Reid 2003: 128)

> 'The question of the archive is not a question of the past; it is not the question of a concept dealing with the past that might already be at our disposal […] It is the question of the future … itself, the question of response, of a promise, and of a responsibility for tomorrow. The archive: if we wanna (sic) know what it will have meant, we will only know in times to come; not tomorrow but in times to come; later on or perhaps never.'
>
> Jacques Derrida, quoted in *Derrida* (Kirby Dick and Amy Ziering, 2002)

The meaning of Rithy Panh's work on the Cambodian genocide[1] is at the confluence of his erstwhile Asio-Diasporic refugee (to France) status, and French and Asian documentary filmmaking practices as well as Panh's own attempts to excavate the future of Cambodia by filming its recent history.[2]

---

1 The International Genocide Convention of 1948 defines genocide 'as various acts such as "killing members of the group" pursued with an intent to destroy, in whole or in part, a national, ethnical, racial or religious group, as such' (Kiernan 2002: 463).
2 This began in 1989 with *Site 2*, a film about Cambodians in refugee camps in Thailand.

For nearly two decades, Panh has made fiction and documentary films on Cambodia.[3] Three of these films deal directly with the Khmer Rouge-perpetrated genocide: *Bophana, a Cambodian Tragedy* (1996), a documentary that recovers the Cambodian people's tragedy during the Khmer Rouge regime; *The People of Angkhor* (2004); and *S21: la machine de mort khmer rouge* (*S21: The Khmer Rouge Killing Machine*, 2002).[4] I have singled out *S21* from Panh's work because it is a Derridaian archive – i.e. one dealing with 'the question of the future ... itself, the question of response [...] and of a responsibility for tomorrow' – pointing towards 'times to come' through a documentary voice mixing the oral and the written, role reversals, claustrophobic space, as well as motionless and silenced memories. The film invokes the mechanics of a major factory of human destruction – S-21 or Tuol Sleng prison – through former prisoners, and guards/torturers/killers,[5] brought together to excavate the future of a present hindered by an unresolved silence on the genocide.

Panh became an Asio-Diasporic refugee in 1980 when he arrived in France at age fifteen, via the Mairut refugee camp in Thailand. He was still running away from a regime that had claimed his parents' and sisters' lives alongside millions of other Cambodians' through starvation, exhaustion and various other forms of torture (see Rollet 2004). In 1985, Panh passed the entrance exam to France's *Institut des hautes études cinématographiques* (IDHEC, now FEMIS) to study filmmaking. That same year, a series of challenges began to unfold in, and take unprecedented proportions for, French documentary: technical innovations like mini-DV cameras, transnational filmmaking practices (for example, at Arté) and French documentary's so-called transformation from exoticist (read 'imperial-' and 'colonial-'minded) collection of 'other' world/international memories in its early years to a non-exoticist depository of the same memories (see Gauthier 2004). Similar challenges would also affect the Asian documentary canon – especially South

---

3   Panh does not make films 'about Cambodia' because, in his view, such films have 'nothing to do with Cambodians, could have been shot anywhere, [as if] you are in Cambodia just for the setting (décor)' (Blum-Reid 2003: 125, quoting Panh.)

4   All translations from French to English in this essay are the author's.

5   'S-21' hyphenated designates the physical prison, and I use it interchangeably with 'Tuol Sleng'. I do not separate guards from torturers and killers because of their collective responsibility in what happened during the Cambodian genocide in general, and at S-21 in particular.

Korean, Japanese and Chinese – with which Panh's work shares interests in seeking to link film subject and filmmaker's existence (which includes the legacy of a turbulent history), as well as in foregrounding the question of the personal film.

Thus, as we shall see, Panh's film work on Cambodia would be part of two sets of issues simultaneously: on the one hand, the changing context of French documentary filmmaking and, on the other, representational and stylistic interests emanating from the Asian documentary canon.

Consequently, here I have two main objectives. Firstly, to locate Panh within the vortex of forced migration, the French and Asian documentary canons, and issues of territory and Panh's geocultural link[6] to the Cambodian genocide. Secondly, to investigate Panh's labour on memory vis-à-vis this genocide, namely the re-constitution of collective memory and the search for the 'real' at play in *S21: The Khmer Rouge Killing Machine*.

In order to investigate Panh's re-constitution of memory and search for the 'real', I will unpick the process by which he translates souvenir into memory in *S21*. 'Souvenir' stands for the perception of events from and through which memory occurs and is formulated into sites – mental and/or physical. In the context of genocide, a souvenir can be a vestige, a trace, and an incomplete archive; hence the translation of souvenir into memory being a re-constitution. I will conceptualise this translation, and name and locate the 'real' he searches for in *S21*. This task entails, in turn, the disjointing of two paths or 'dead ends' according to Emmanuel Burdeau (2004b: 15), in relation to *S21*: on the one hand *'le travail du film'*/the work of the film (alluding to the filmmaking process) and, on the other hand, the result of filming (the film itself)/*'travail filmé'*. Leaping out of the two paths, I will locate the 'real' of *S21* at their borders. As a result, documentary form will be questioned, the gap between *S21* and the subject/s it documents analysed, and the boundaries between documentary subjects (i.e. genocide, S-21, former prisoners and guards/torturers/killers) and *documenteur* (Panh) investigated.

---

6   I adopt 'geocultural' to refer to 'commonalities of language and culture' as used by Jean K. Shalaby in her study of media transnationalism: 'the process of media globalisation involves the formation of a second international layer that fits between the national and global levels: the geocultural region' (2005: 4).

Locating Rithy Panh: Forced Migration, Filmmaking, Geoculture

The American escalation of the war in Vietnam and endless carpet bombings of Cambodia's countryside and its border with Vietnam culminated in President Richard Nixon's decision to invade Cambodia in May 1970. By the time Congress put a halt to bombings in 1973, 540,000 tons of bombs had been dropped on Cambodia. There were '130,000 new Khmer refugees'; sixty per cent of refugees surveyed in Cambodia's towns blamed American bombings as 'the main cause of their displacement' (Kiernan 2002: 19). (Of course, Cambodia has this in common with other region of Asia such as Vietnam and Korea.)

President Nixon and Secretary of State Henry Kissinger were directly responsible for Pol Pot's seizure of power from Lon Nol's pro-American military regime. Pol Pot's Communist Party of Kampuchea (CPK) rose from the devastation of rural Cambodia. The CPK manipulated the American massacre of civilian populations for propaganda and recruitment purposes, using both to justify violent and extreme CPK policies. For example, CPK cadres told young peasant victims that the planes came from Phnom Penh and, by the same token, made 'The popular outrage over the US bombing [...] fatal for the two million inhabitants of Phnom Penh' (Kiernan 2002: 25). As CPK troops evacuated Phnom Penh by force in 1975, they told its urban population – including Panh at age eleven and his family – that the mass departure to the countryside was needed because American B-52 planes were on the verge of bombing the city. The first of Panh's three-phase escape from Cambodia was complete.

Panh's migrant body cannot be located effectively unless one understands two of the Pol Pot regime's most dominant themes: race, and the fight for central power (or top-down domination). Khmer Rouge perceptions of race eclipsed those of class because Pol Pot and his associates were from privileged backgrounds, with no experience of peasant life. They disregarded an alternative leadership from grassroots background and, increasingly, reduced the top CPK circle to 'the French-educated Pol Pot group' (Kiernan 2002: 26). Khmer Rouge perceptions of race also eclipsed organisational necessities: 'non-Khmer Cambodians with extensive revolutionary experience and CPK seniority were removed from the leadership and usually murdered' (*Ibid.*).

The Pol Pot regime was racist and conducted neither a proletarian revolution (favouring the working class) nor a peasant revolution (privileging all farmers). As a case in point, non-Khmers dominated the peasantry and were singled out 'for persecution because of their race' (*Ibid.*). Similarly, although the Khmers were the 'single approved' and favoured race in Democratic Kampuchea,[7] being Khmer was insufficient for 'official approval': you could be arrested, forcibly moved, tortured and/or killed like any other ethnic-minority Cambodian. The country's political diversity and ethnic heterogeneity were challenges to which CPK leaders opposed a successful terrorising top-down domination of party and country: 'Enemies were thus, by definition, everywhere' (Kiernan 2002: 27).

> A whole nation was kidnapped and then besieged from within. … Human communication almost disappeared. Democratic Kampuchea was a prison camp state, and the eight million prisoners served most of their time in solitary confinement. And 1.5 million of the inmates were worked, starved, and beaten to death.
>
> The vicious silence of Democratic Kampuchea tolled in the late twentieth century … For Cambodia was sealed off. …. Worse … people were reduced to their daily instructions. Memory was as dangerous as drinking milk. (Kiernan 2002: 8–9)

Whether the victims featured in *S21*, and Panh and his family, were Khmer or not made no difference: they were bound for entrapment by a racist regime attempting to re-write Cambodian history through ethnic cleansing. Consequently, the Rithy Panh who reached France at age fifteen embodied forced migration and displacement. As a body thrice removed from Cambodia – Phnom Penh to the Cambodian countryside, to Thailand, to France – Panh was always going to have to engage with three issues: ideas of home/host country, the Khmer Rouge attempt to re-write Cambodian history, and being an Asio-Diasporic refugee.[8] This, I would suggest, is the context within which Panh's continuous attempts to facilitate dialogue on memory

---

7   The name given to Cambodia under the Pol Pot regime.
8   For example, for ten years, 1979–89, Panh refused to return to Cambodia and even stopped speaking his mother tongue (see Blum-Reid 2003: 109).

and his search for the 'real' of the genocide must be understood.

Filmmaking is Panh's chosen craft for his *'travail sur la mémoire'*/'labour on memory' which is about documenting lived experiences and re-establishing communication about genocide between victims. He admits that if the Cambodian genocide had not taken place and he stayed in Cambodia he would not have been a cineaste (Panh 2004: 15). Thus, his own lived experience as a migrant and Asio-Diasporic refugee in France significantly influenced his decision to take up filmmaking. So too did Panh's need to re-establish communication about the genocide between Cambodians themselves on the one hand, and between Cambodian and other world memories of similar trauma on the other.

Guy Gauthier's claim that French documentary became a non-exoticist depository of 'other' world memories helps locate Panh's documentary work on Cambodia within a French canon of documentary filmmaking – at the levels of production, representation and interest in universal human rights – which stretches as far back as Jean Rouch's mid-1950s-to-early-1960s aesthetic of 'revelation'. According to this aesthetic, the camera is 'a valuable catalytic agent' in which 'one seldom senses the director' (Barnouw 1993: 253, 254). Panh's direct connection to this canon stems from Marcel Ophüls' radical questioning of the myth of the French *Résistance* in *Le Chagrin et la Pitié* (*The Sorrow and the Pity*, 1971), a film released during a decade that witnessed French documentary's attempt to reconcile 'act of creation' and 'search for truth' with modesty (Gauthier 2004: 155). Ophüls and partner Andrew Harris are credited with introducing 'the witness' who 'was there' with her/his 'subjectivity' and her/his 'motivations' into a cinema 'turned towards the past'. Gauthier goes on to suggest that this type of witness caused 'the historical film [to] leave much room for the film about memory' to develop (2004: 175).

S21 bears witness to Panh's adoption of the Ophülsian witness; the film about memory; and a filmic practice seeking humility and, to a lesser extent, truth. Simultaneously, however, there are differences between his approach and the French documentary canon. For example, unlike Ophüls, Panh searches for the 'real' but does not mistrust his witnesses. Furthermore, picturing the French canon's so-called embrace of 'all the memories of the world', using colonial and paternalistic vocabulary,[9] tends to overlook crucial issues, such as how these Other-ed postcolonial memories and cineastes actively enrich the French documentary; and how they contribute, from the outside-in, to trans-nationalise this documentary canon through the work of geoculture. Geoculture escapes the 'national' in time and space. Geoculture also allows (dis)placed individuals and communities to connect to several cultures simultaneously.[10] Thus, by virtue of both his status of Francophone filmmaker of Cambodian/South-East Asian origin and Asio-Diasporic refugee, Panh can be located vis-à-vis another, trans-national, canon of filmmaking: the Asian documentary.[11]

Panh shares with Asian documentary filmmakers a tendency to search for points of connection between 'their own existence' and the subject of their films (see Yano 2004: 26); examples would include Kim Dong-won (South Korea) whose *A Repatriation* (2003) is about a North Korean spy imprisoned in South Korea, and Wu Yii-feng (Taiwan) whose *Gift of Life* (2003) deals with the September 1999 earthquake in Taiwan. Panh's links to the Asian documentary canon go even further as he makes films that are less about revealing the truth than about what Yano Kazuyuki calls 'the cineaste's problematic relation to a subject'. *S21* is not about the filmmaker merely looking at/treating a given subject matter. Rather, filmmaker and subject matter seem to collaborate in order to create the film itself and therefore, quoting Yano in another context, 'shooting transforms the film being made, adding tension to the directing process itself' (2004: 26): examples would include documentaries focusing on Asian genocides such as Nanjing, and those by Japanese filmmakers such as Kamanaka Hitomi's *Hibakusha: At The End of the World* (2003) a film on Hiroshima's survivors, Mori Tatsuya's *A* (1998) or *A2* (2001) on the Aoum sect, and Hara Kazuo's *The Emperor's Army Marches On* (1987) where 62-year-old Japanese war veteran Okuzaki

---

9   'It [the French documentary] has taken on', or is 'always willing to welcome cineastes who have come from far away' (Gauthier 2004: 186).
10 Geoculture theory should also alert critics, such as Sylvie E. Blum-Reid (2003: 121), to the dangers of seeing Panh's so-called cultural attachments as limited to the binary Cambodia–France.
11 Panh shares such a location with exilic and diasporic French filmmakers of Vietnamese origin, such as Lam Lê (*Poussière d'Empire/Dust of Empire*, 1983), Dzu le Lieu (*Les Hommes des trois Ky/The Men of the Three Ky*, 1996) or Tran Anh Hung (*L'Odeur de la papaye verte/The Scent of Green Papaya*, 1993).

Kenzo, who is haunted by memories of fellow soldiers murdered and eaten by Japanese officers in New Guinea during World War II, campaigns to reveal the truth about it. Last but not least, Panh's connection to the Asian documentary runs through the idea of the personal film, which is characteristic of the work of Chinese filmmakers Wang Bing – for example *A l'Ouest des Rails* (*The Other Side of the Tracks*, 2003), about a town's slow process of decay – or Zhong Hua with *This Winter* (2001).

In summary then, thanks to geoculture, Panh is located at once between and within the French and the Asian documentary canons. Thus, Panh's seemingly obsessive return to the Cambodian genocide belies a personal quest for a 'home' (Cambodia) that can only be a host country or culture at best. Similarly, this return to the genocide and to Cambodia is done from a host country/culture/refuge (France) that cannot really be 'home' for Panh: after all, from 1863, well before the US bombed Cambodia and Vietnam invaded it, the country 'had been mummified by ninety years of a French colonial protectorate ... France walled Cambodia off from other foreign influences ... until French rule in Indochina broke down [in the 1950s]' (Kiernan 2002: 4–5). It follows that Panh's Asio-Diasporic refugee body, even though re-territorialised within France/the French documentary, constantly returns to its primal moment, the Cambodian genocide, an indirect result of the French colonial mummification of Cambodia.[12] In short, Panh is a decentred body whose identity is floating (not drifting) on a kaleidoscopic cultural sea between Europe and South East Asia.

Genocide, Memory and the Naming of the 'Real'

According to the International Genocide Convention's definition, the Pol Pot regime's totalitarian politics and racist project of ethnic cleansing in Cambodia were genocide. The nature of the memory rising from the dust of Democratic Kampuchea is a cluster of silent souvenirs of systematic de-

---

12 This is further complicated by the fact that Panh's work is not solely on Cambodia. His second film is a portrait of veteran Malian filmmaker Souleymane Cissé: *Souleymane Cissé: Cinéaste de notre temps* (1991); while *Que la barque se brise, que la jonque s'entrouvre* (*Let the Boat Break*) (shot in 2000) looks at trauma among Asian refugees in France. The latter film is the first one attempting to reconcile Vietnamese and Cambodian refugee communities in France (see Blum-Reid 2003: 117).

struction locked within the survivors' bodies. Consequently, in order to undo the silence and unlock the souvenirs, a process of transforming souvenir into memory must take place. As we shall see *S21* illustrate, such a process involves filmmaker and (other) survivors facing difficult tasks vis-à-vis the Cambodian genocide, namely putting ex-torturers in a position to recover memory while deprogramming ex-victims' memory from belief in Khmer Rouge 'truth' and threat. The aim of the filmmaker must therefore be to reach a space where, in Panh's words, 'victim and torturer need one another to continue together the work of memory' (in Rollet 2004: 25). In other words, memory is conceived as a nurturer of history, and the work of memory cannot take place without reviving the wounds of a tumultuous history for therapeutic purposes. Not only is this the challenge for *S21*, it is also the process through which we can name the 'real' Panh is looking for. In documentary/film, the 'real' is multifaceted, and can be one or all of the following: 'product or residue'; gap between documentary/cinema and what it documents; born of 'friction'; going against the general trend; no more than 'difference, contradiction or montage' (see Burdeau 2004: 15).

The 'real' Rithy Panh searches for, the logic that informs *S21*, is framed by three key words: unpredictability, possibility, and the irreparable. According to Marie-José Mondzain, in his three films on Cambodia, Panh's 'paradoxical deployment of the unpredictable and the possible at the centre of the irreparable itself' is striking (2004: 23). This seeming paradox can, in fact, be explained by a Buddhist belief imbedded in Cambodian culture and language (Cambodia is roughly eighty per cent Buddhist): the continuous variation or transformation of destinies and stories. 'Here, the real is forever enriched or open to enrichment by the possible'; 'Everything can disappear while nothing dies' (*Ibid.*). Therefore, the 'real' Panh searches for would need to be triggered in formerly-silenced bodies, i.e. the survivors'. Its continuous process of mutation must also be tracked and accounted for through *all* survivors' memories as well as contemporary documentary filmmaking (the possible). In this line of thought, the disappeared/dead of the Cambodian genocide pass on and get reincarnated into new shapes. Everything and everyone about the genocide has its importance because the 'real' transcends cultural and linguistic differences within Cambodia. The 'real' also rises above Khmer Rouge attempts to eradicate Cambodia's spiritual sustenance:

Buddhism (see Kiernan 2002: 55–8 for the Khmer rouge persecution of Buddhists). This in turn calls for a complex documentary film device to tell what can only be described as a multifaceted and difficult story. Panh provides such a device in *S21* and we need to disjoint the film in order to locate and describe the 'real' of the genocide.

S21 Disjointed: Locating and Describing the 'Real'

Looking to draw a line between 'reality' and 'fiction' in documentary representation is futile, if not obsolete.[13] The question of documentary form, however, is still a pertinent one not least because of possibilities offered by technical innovations such as light weight DV cameras and individual filmmakers' choices of re-presentation.

Documentary form now embodies an improvisatory potential that *S21* illustrates well. Rather than offer a straightforward ethnographic approach to the Cambodian genocide, Panh's film endlessly replays portions of this genocide in order to re-construct the 'real', complicating documentary form in the same process. As a result, in order to turn catastrophe into possibility, the work of *S21*/'*travail du film*' frees its own diegesis, 'reversing and making signs of the labour travel between the subjects [that *S21* films]' (Burdeau 2004: 15).

There is no respect of documentary formal traditions in Panh's film. As we shall see, repetitive re-enactments, by former S-21 guards/torturers/killers, of the language and gestures used against prisoners come unannounced, have no logic. And yet, through '*travail filmé*', repetitive re-enactments give responsibility and freedom to the former guards/torturers/killers of S-21 to engage with their victims in the work of memory. It follows that this complex combination of lack of logic on the one hand and handover of responsibility and freedom on the other reiterate why '*travail du film*' and '*travail filmé*' are, traditionally speaking, dead ends to be transcended in order to effectively locate and describe the 'real' in *S21*. To achieve this, let us look at (the) three ways in which *S21* interrogates documentary form: repetitive re-enactments, role reversals, and the use of still photography.

---

13 For example, see Ward 2005: 31–48, and the very useful work of Bill Nichols, for example *Representing Reality* (1991) or *Introduction to Documentary* (2001).

S21 interrogates documentary form through repetitive re-enactments whose oral, sonic and pantomimic emphases create representational cracks that allow the 'real' to emerge. For example, taking sequences featuring the empty rooms of Tuol Sleng prison, I would suggest that anytime a guard/torturer/killer walks in them to mime violent acts and/or speak, his freedom to terrorise prisoners and the latter's suffering become visible. The guard/torturer/killer's present, corporeal voice is echoed by the absent but immortal voices of the tortured: presence meets absence, speech speaks to silence, 'everything disappears but nothing dies', and the full picture of the horror is revealed.

S21 interrogates documentary form through role reversal: former victims interrogate former interrogators. The process forces the latter to take responsibility for what happened at Tuol Sleng. It is also an opportunity for the only two S-21 survivors still alive – painter Vann Nath, and Chhum Hey – to dismantle their former interrogators' memories.[14] Panh's purpose, I would argue, is to achieve something unachievable through traditional interviews. This is because, as a text, *S21* is dismantling the Khmer Rouge machine whose essence was to 'change memory, to end up making both instruments and victims of the machine believe what the regime claimed to be the truth' (Rollet 2004: 24). Thus, *S21* offers another form of taking responsibility: healing and, eventually, reconciliation. Unlike landmark treatments of genocide in documentary film, such as Claude Lanzmann's *Shoah* (1985) on the Jewish Holocaust, Panh's *S21* does not 'preserve' the past as the 'insurmountable, incomparable … passage of [the Cambodian genocide] ordeal'. For Lanzmann, the 'real' (i.e. 'the past' in *Shoah*) cannot be reduced to the question of what is possible and what is not or to 'the present' (see Mondzain 2004: 22); the Holocaust is a 'crime, violence, trauma', 'irretrievably located in the past' and therefore inaccessible. Lanzmann does not so much 'represent the past as he reactivate[s] it in images of the present' (Williams 1998: 389). This, combined with Lanzmann's desire to preserve the past, explains why he 'refused to use a single image of atrocities or physical suffering and has avoided the use of archival material' (Bresheeth 2006: 58).[15] In *Shoah* memory does not come through souvenir – it rejects souve-

---

14 Out of 14,000 prisoners held at S-21, only seven escaped execution.
15 On the other hand, Panh opens *S21* with a panning panoramic shot of contemporary Phnom Penh and then cuts to archival newsreel footage of Democratic Kampuchea propaganda.

nir – and as a result the film allows no diegetic space for still photographs. *S21* on the other hand uses still photography to look at genocide, pain and, in the same process, to interrogate documentary form. When documentary film deals with genocide, memory and mourning, working with photography means working with vestiges or traces because photography lacks memory:

> Nothing of the memory of those photographed is from then on present on the photograph. Photography fixes a trace without memory, a souvenir that belongs to the photographer who would like nonetheless that his souvenir becomes memory for others. (Mondzain 2004: 22)

Working with photography in this context also means having to choose types of photography. *S21* focuses on the mug shot because it was the Khmer Rouge's favoured visual archive (14,000 such shots taken at Tuol Sleng). They used it in combination with written 'confessions' in order to forcibly construct memory for viewers 'in times to come'. Of course, these mug shots make subjects look threatening, dangerous, suspicious and/or an enemy. The mug shots signify also the representation of 'Time', the imminence of the prisoners' death or a Barthesian *punctum* also known as the sting that captures the viewer's attention from an image (Barthes 2000: 96). As contemporary viewers, we know that mug shot subjects are dead and that, at the time the photographs were taken, they were about to die.

However, I would suggest that through Vann Nath, Chhum Hey,[16] and Tuol Sleng prison personnel featured in *S21* (particularly photographer Nhem En) Panh asks how *punctum* will operate throughout the process of his labouring on memory and the Cambodian genocide. I would also suggest, our direct viewing relationship to the mug shots notwithstanding, that Panh understands that Time is not static. Indeed, he does not use photographs in the traditional and one-dimensional sense of illustrating visually the documentary's aural track, or as props. Rather, Panh transforms photographs into points of departure so that the viewer can see the work of Time, the intersection of signs/discourses within and between photographs.

---

16 Nath and Hey broke the cycle of death. Their survival makes them exceptions to the rule of imminent death captured on the mug shot.

In this line of thought, Panh makes contemporary viewers – Tuol Sleng victims included – see what Barthes calls '*This will be* and *this has been* ... an anterior future of which death is the stake ... a defeat of Time' (2000: 96). At the same time, Panh adds three other dimensions of Time for contemporary viewers to see: this had been, this will have been, and what will this be/ what will this mean?

'What will this be/what will this mean?' refers to the extent to which the S-21 photographic archive can potentially advance Panh's future work on memory. Indeed, in *S21* Panh demonstrates that each of the 14,000 shots is a place of memory, and that each photograph shows an individual on whom work is to be done 'in times to come'. As we can see from the image below, Panh's camera attempts to capture each and every face. In the film, Panh's camera moves slowly from left to right and closes up on three mug shots of girls whose gaze can be distinctly seen by the viewer. The point of this panning shot is suggested by Panh's own comment that 'in a genocide, anonymity is an accomplice of erasure' (Panh 2004: 15). Thus, according to Panh's

Courtesy of MK2 Productions; special thanks to Ariane Engel

film style and use of still photography, viewers must see all the victims as distinct individuals: this is what the photographs will be/will mean, something consistent with *S21* being a Derridaian archive that we may never fully know. Last but not least, the interior architecture of Tuol Sleng, the dozens of photographs hanging on the walls within large frames and the position of Panh's camera collectively produce a natural deep focus effect, as well as reiterate his acknowledgement of the magnitude of the genocide and the work yet to be done on it.

Returning to the complex documentary device I am analysing (*'travail du film'* and *'travail filmé'*), I would suggest after, Emmanuel Burdeau (2004: 15), that for a long time documentary/cinema has been in an either/or position vis-à-vis these two categories. Either it assumed its ability to have 'good faith', to demonstrate its own honesty and to declare itself 'the defence and illustration of an adequate method' of capturing reality, or it dwelled on the illusion that cinema, premising on filming something fundamentally different from itself, will 'only [discover] ... itself, [and] the omnipresence of play and *mise-en-scene*' at the end of this process. Leaping out of these two dead ends, i.e. not being bogged down by formalism, reveals the 'real' at their interstice. As mentioned earlier, in *S21* the 'real' takes on various meanings one can gather in two distinct but interconnected threads: issues of terror, emancipation and freedom on the one hand, responsibility and reconciliation on the other.

As a case in point, early in the film, the sequence featuring Him Houy[17] with his parents and children show that the 'real' is in a space from which *'travail du film'* and *'travail filmé'* cannot extract it. This space is timeless, or time-resistant: the future (for example, Houy's wife and children) and the past (Houy's parents' belief in his innocence, in bad Karma and exorcism) are still grappling with a present and unchanging state (i.e. Houy's). In this space/in Houy's state, terror cannot be disappeared (in the Buddhist sense invoked earlier) despite the fact that twenty years have passed since the Khmer Rouge regime fell. Emancipation or freedom cannot yet be achieved either. The result of all this is that separating *'travail du film'* from *'travail filmé'* allows us to locate the 'real', be able to describe it as locked in Houy's

---

17 He is the first ex-guard/torturer/killer shown, although we don't know this yet.

body and mind (Houy blames Khmer Rouge leaders for his actions) and, therefore, can only be engaged with 'in times to come'. In other words, this 'real' is a residue at the edge of *S21*'s frame, in future encounters between Panh's camera and Houy beyond *S21*.

It is in this context of postponement that viewers of *S21* can understand the frustration and pain of victims Chhum Hey and Vann Nath when they try to make sense of the genocide in order to actually begin the dialogic work of reconciliation:

Hhey: I hear rumours according to which we need to have reconciliation, bury the resentment. Nath, what do you think of the idea of putting Pol Pot and the Khmer Rouge on trial?

Nath: Reconciliation ... They can do what they want. But until now has anyone said this past action was wrong? Has anyone begged forgiveness? Have you heard that from the lips of the leaders or underlings?

Hhey: No.

Nath: Me neither. So how can we help the families of victims and survivors find peace again?

Hhey: Everybody dodges saying they're not guilty.[18] What do we do?

Nath: I don't want revenge against these people. But to tell us to forget because it belongs to the past ... This is something painful, really painful and even if it's been twenty years it's not so far back. It hasn't 'dried'.

Hhey: So long as I live, nothing will be erased.

The lack of repentance or recognition of wrong-doing from top Khmer Rouge leaders (and underlings) alive in 2002, the work of Time, as well as successive governments' attempt to erase the issue of Khmer Rouge genocide from Cambodian national consciousness make the location of Hhey and Nath's 'real' difficult. What is 'real' for them goes beyond the moment of genocide. Panh and *S21* cannot provide answers to Hhey and Nath's questions, for Hhey and Nath's 'real' is part of a more complex 'real' for

---

18 According to Panh (2004: 17), after seeing *S21*, Khmer Rouge leader and former Democratic Kamputchea President Khieu Samphan recognised that Tuol Sleng was 'indeed a state institution' but added that he 'had never known beforehand what had taken place there. He was discovering suddenly that it was a planned genocide'.

which Panh is still searching today. Besides, as we know, Panh puts Hhey and Nath *en scene* for them to explore ways out of their respective impasses and, as we shall see, this complicated situation is further compounded by Panh the *documenteur*'s complex connection to memory, the 'real', and the subject matter and subjects (i.e. individuals) in *S21*.

Documenteur and Documentary Subject/s: Gap or Blurred Boundaries?

In effect, the device Panh uses in *S21* detaches him from the subject matter and the subjects he documents in the film. As a case in point, it is Vann Nath who interrogates the ex-guards/torturers/killers: Panh is not seen or heard in the film. His intervention is at non-diegetic level, a meta-level discourse.[19]

Simultaneously, however, Panh's directorial detachment emphasises how his boundaries and those of the subject matter and the subjects in *S21* are blurred. He is an archivist who 'inhabits the [Cambodian] archive as both producer and product of the archive, as both a determining and a determined force ... a shaper also contained by the ideology he ... inscribes for future memory' (Smith 2004: 156). In other words, Panh is, at once, a *victim* of the Pol Pot regime; a (former) political and (current) cultural *refugee* to France with strong geocultural connections to Cambodia; an Asio-Diasporic Francophone body (the work he does on memory is personal). This state of affairs explains why he has re-turned to the Cambodian genocide before and after *S21*, and will carry on doing so. It also explains why he refuses to judge the perpetrators of the genocide and/or claim to bring justice to its victims, dead or alive.[20] Panh's ideology as an archivist is about setting in motion a process of healing and an ongoing search for the elusive 'real', without which survival is impossible.

Conclusion

Rithy Panh's work on the Khmer Rouge-perpetrated Cambodian genocide in general and *S21* in particular does not, per se, deal with 'the past that

---

19 See also Blum-Reid (2003: 115–16) on Panh's filmic approach: 'Panh professes to observe Cambodian people and their daily life from the inside ... The voice is given to the people.'
20 Panh refused to let *S21* be used as evidence in trials (see Mondzain 2004: 24).

might already be at our disposal. It is a question of the future'; like a Derrid-aian archive, the full meanings of Panh's (de-)construction/re-construction of memory, his search for the 'real' of the genocide, as well as Panh's floating Cambodian-Francophone identity are always-already to come. At this stage in his career, Panh gathers dust in the wind: there is no way of knowing for certain which way/s this wind will blow, and/or how strongly. The only certainty is that he re-turns to the Cambodian genocide in order to excavate the future of his native land. Panh's *Le papier ne peut pas enveloper la braise* (2006, released in France in March 2007) focuses on the plight of child and adolescent female prostitutes in Phnom Penh. Although the film seems to make no direct connections between prostitution and the Cambodian geno-cide, I could not help but notice that one of the places where the prostitutes ply their trade is located in front of the barbed-wired S-21 building.

Bibliography

Bailey, David A. and Stuart Hall (2003) 'The Vertigo of Displacement', in Liz Wells (ed.) *The Photography Reader*. London: Routledge, 380–6.

Barnouw, Erik (1993) *Documentary: A History of the Non-Fiction Film*, New York: Oxford University Press.

Barthes, Roland (2000) *Camera Lucida: Reflections on Photography*. Trans. Richard Howard. London: Vintage.

Blum-Reid, Sylvie (2003) *East-West Encounters: Franco-Asian Cinema and Literature*. London: Wallflower Press.

Bresheeth, Haim. (2006) 'Projecting Trauma: War Photography and the *Public Sphere*', *Third Text*, 20, 1, 57–71.

Burdeau, Emmanuel (2004a) 'Au nom de l'inquiétude', *Cahiers du cinéma*, February, 587, 10–11.

____ (2004b) 'Réel: la bonne nouvelle', *Cahiers du cinéma*, October, 594, 12–15.

Chandler, David (1999) *Voices from S-21: Terror and History in Pol Pot's Secret Prison*. Berkeley, Los Angeles, and London: University of California Press.

Frodon, Jean-Michel (2004) 'Juste des images', *Cahiers du cinéma*, February, 587, 19–20, 22.

____ (2007) 'Les formes de la douleur', *Cahiers du cinéma*, April, 622, 45–6.

Gauthier, Guy (2004) *Un siècle de documentaires français: des tourneurs de manivel-*

les aux voltigeurs du multimédia. Paris: Armand Collin.

Kiernan, Ben (2002) *The Pol Pot Regime; Race, Power, and Genocide under the Khmer Rouge, 1975–79*, second edition. New Haven, CT and London: Yale University Press.

Mangeot, Philippe (2004) 'Une cérémonie', *Cahiers du cinéma*, February, 587, 18.

Mondzain, Marie-Jose (2004) 'Photos souvenirs et cinéma mémoire', *Cahiers du cinéma*, October, 594, 22–4.

Nichols, Bill (1991) *Representing Reality : Issues and Concepts in Documentary*, USA : Indiana University Press.

____ (2002) *Introduction to Documentary*, USA : Indiana University Press.

Panh, Rithy (2004) '"Je suis un arpenteur de mémoires"', *Cahiers du cinéma*, February, 587, 14–17.

Rehm, Jean-Pierre (2004) 'Fabrique de mémoire contre machine de mort', *Cahiers du cinéma*, February, 587, 12–13.

Rollet, Sylvie (2004) '*S21, la machine de mort khmère rouge*: un génocide à hauteur d'homme', *Positif*, Février, 516, 24–5.

Shalaby, Jean K. (ed.) (2005) *Transnational Television Worldwide: Towards a New Media Order*. London: I. B. Tauris.

Smith, Sean-Michelle (2004) *Photography on the Color Line: W. E. B. Du Bois and the Paris 1900 Exposition*. Durham, NC and London: Duke University Press.

Yano, Kazuyuki (2004) 'Survol du documentaire asiatique'. Trans. Mikiko Tomita, *Cahiers du cinéma*, October, 594, 26.

Ward, Paul (2005) *Documentary: The Margins of Reality*. London: Wallflower Press.

Williams, Linda (1998) 'Mirrors Without Memories: Truth, History, and *The Thin Blue Line*', in Bill Nichols, Barry Keith Grant, Jeanette Sloniowski (eds) *Documenting the Documentary*. Detroit: Wayne State University Press, 379–96.

Black Hole In the Sky, Total Eclipse Under the Ground: Apichatpong Weerasethakul and the Ontological Turn of Cinema

Seung-hoon Jeong

Although already hailed as a promising Asian maestro, Apichatpong Weerasethakul has introduced to international audiences a series of works which are difficult to tag appropriately. Not only his debut feature *Mysterious Object at Noon* (2000), but the subsequent *Blissfully Yours* (2002) and Cannes-endorsed *Tropical Malady* (2004), are full of mysterious, blissful and tropical sunshine. They all exude 'indexical' (state of affairs) images typical of Third World cinema, with traces of a long underdeveloped but now globalised Southeast Asia, with amateur actors wandering through jungle, border areas and urban streets, yet no label such as 'neo-realist, documentary-tinted national cinema' can fully capture their strange freshness. Nor does it suffice to say that the Apichatpong world fills such a frame of cinematic reference with indigenous legends and narrative experiments, including the surrealist 'exquisite corpse'[1] and bipartite structure. Nor can film buffs grasp his philosophical long take by invoking Hou Hsiao-Hsien or Bela

---

1   Exquisite corpse (also known as 'exquisite cadaver' or 'rotating corpse') is a method by which a collection of words or images are collectively assembled, the result being known as 'cadavre exquis' in French. Each collaborator adds to a composition in sequence, either by following a rule (for example, 'The adjective noun adverb verb the adjective noun') or by being allowed to see the end of what the previous person contributed.

Tarr, and his architectural tracking shot by comparing it to that of Stanley Kubrick or Alain Resnais. What kind of love on earth do his love stories depict? Does his gay romance have any political nuance of New Queer Cinema? All these uncharted 'syndromes' of a new cinematic 'century' in the wake of the so-called 'death of cinema' driven by digital media might only be attributed to an 'Apichatpong genre'. This is not a title that can be granted to any auteur. Ultimately, he seems to funnel various temporal strata of film experiments – from fixed shot to tracking shot, from pan or zoom to montage – and their theoretical implications in film history – into an idiosyncratic cinematic space, while transforming them into cinematic memories that reside inherently in it. So the viewer is urged to become not only a geographer and aesthetician, but geologist and archeologist of cinema.

In order to venture into the immanent territory of memory, let us start from his actual profilmic territory, which in any case deserves a geopolitical 'cognitive mapping'. For his characters' relationships are not coalesced so much as disseminated over spaces, through which a presumed fictional world often dissolves into the real world where a film is shot. Look back at *Mysterious Object at Noon*, whose collective storytelling never hinders the ethnographic camera from witnessing the raw reality surrounding a fish peddler, political posters, news of Japan and America, and so forth, along the path from the countryside to Bangkok. How about *Blissfully Yours*, a dangerous love story of a Thai girl and a Burmese immigrant in the border region surrounding an anonymous city and its forested suburbs? This backdrop evolves in even more detail in *Tropical Malady*. What we see through the shy gay couple's slightly euphoric meanderings and loss-search narrative is not an organic romantic progression, but the dispersed urban space with multilayered temporality; not an Antonioni-style modernist journey, but the postmodern synchronicity of non-synchronous times in which eternal premodernity coexists with belated modernisation and timely globalisation, with shamanist Buddhism sitting side by side with the Thai rock band 'Clash' and a kitch techno. This 'vernacular modernism' derived from that of the West – namely, a double vernacularisation – could not better epitomise the world system 'remediated' by Thailand.

Historical signs and their textual spatiality are more salient in the two discrete parts of *Syndromes and a Century* (2006). Given the film's original plan of recalling a love story between the director's doctor parents, the distance between the rural and urban areas insinuates the gap between the 1970s, spent in his parents' hospitals, and the new century he now inhabits. It is this space-time entanglement that marks the shift from the tranquil, humorous first half to the somewhat chilly, ultramodern second half. The surreal harmony of a huge Buddhist statue and a basketball hoop is thus replaced by the real contrast of a Buddhist statue dwarfed by elevated roads and the bronze statues of modern people. Photos of a new-tech industrial area that Dr Nohng's girlfriend shows in the hope of living there represent nothing so much as indexes of Southeast Asia's transformation into a place prefigured in Antonioni's *Red Desert* (1964) with such overwhelming, even sublime factories, albeit without the gloomy smoke. No doubt, Apichatpong's geological observation of multi-temporal space updates and expands the work of contemporary East Asian auteurs such as Edward Yang, Jia Zhangke and, to some extent, Hong Sang-soo.

While encompassing all these references to reality, however, his mapping also opens up unfamiliar dimensions that cannot be interpreted as the conventional postmodern nostalgia for what is lost, or a mere utopian/dystopian vision of the industrialised future. Among these novel aspects is a sort of hyperrealist phenomenology, which other Asian realists have not taken seriously in their cultural studies. When the couple in *Blissfully Yours* make love in the forest, the camera involves us not only in their psychology, but the 'real' 3D space of subtle yet vivid synesthesia which emerges slowly in the form of crisp soil, streaming perspiration, sweet berries, whispering breezes, and twigs scratching skin with its accompanying swelling. Not limited to any socio-historical sign system, such contingent effects of the nature-sense circuit as those reinforced in the dark jungle of *Tropical Malady* leads to a pure audiovisual situation: a non-signifying, material surrounding which is too pure for a modern viewer to experience outside of a darkened theatre, that is, an artificial jungle.

Not surprisingly, the filmmaker with an architecture degree has also been an installation artist whose video works experiment less on the conventional perception of the viewer in a theatre, than on the embodied sensation of the visitor to a museum, an immersive space; the alternative art space that accommodates ever more cineastes working on new media in this post-avant-garde period.

Syndromes and a Century stimulates such immersion through the use of a more social environment. While Hong Sang-soo maintains cynical distance from the characters despite his microscopic interest in mundane life, Apichatpong here attempts a warmer, phenomenological approach to his memory-imbued daily space, with a persistent focus not on characters so much as the atmosphere surrounding them. Without paying attention to speaking faces, his long shot-long take invites us to an ecological space where tropical trees gently sway outside a medical office, and where a young monk plays guitar beside patients chatting peacefully under the afternoon sunshine. When the performance scene – Apichatpong's entertaining signature – of a dentist-singer interrupts the narrative for a time, what the camera presents is not simply a 'cinema of attractions', but the harmonious and ineffable aura that dissolves the entire heterogeneous surrounding containing the ordinary stage and audience, shoppers at a market, and people playing volleyball in a yard. Meanwhile, it is the excessively hygienic interior of the urban hospital that embodies to the utmost a museum-like space, through which the viewer-visitor walks behind a camera that slides over sleek, immaculate corridors and rooms lighted by fluorescent lamps and surrounded by unidentified ambient noises. Even prior to and beyond our recognition of ultra-Westernisation, we become immersed in this glossy labyrinth by virtue of the collective sensation of surface and environmental effects created by artificial light and sound.

However, the hospital which multicoloured uniforms crisscross in perfect order – allegorising an apparently conflict-less society, or multiculturalism? – has a basement evoking von Trier's *The Kingdom* (2004), an uncanny repository of bizarre events including the omen of an apocalyptic catastrophe. Who are that tennis-obsessed patient in this white antiseptic place – like the entrepreneur in Fassbinder's *In a Year of 13 Moons* (1978) – and that female doctor hiding whiskey in a prosthetic limb – like a judge whose book is pornography in Kafka's *The Trial*? But in fact, Apichatpong has little interest in tackling hysteria or hypocrisy of authority. When the middle-aged doctor tries the *chakra* healing under the fluorescent lamp, a folk remedy that involves channeling the sun's power into the body, this is neither an absurd joke nor a satire of superstition, but may be the hint of a link between the natural light shining in Part 1 and its artificial counterpart prevailing in Part 2. The latter does not seem to be a mere reversal or displacement of the former, but urges us to pose a naïve but provocative question: how has the sun been replaced by a fluorescent lamp?

To answer this, we need to take a detour via *Tropical Malady*, which leads us from civilisation back to nature. In particular, when the soldier gropes around the dark stretching all his antennae towards the opulent sound, smell and touch of real nature, the ghost-beast he pursues lurks there, paradoxically, as something that all these saturated senses miss, as a quasi-being that his sensory-motor system fails to capture or barely traces. This is why he comes across a baboon speaking, a dead cow resurrecting, and finally a tiger watching him prior to his discovery of it; the moment that the film leaps from the phenomenological impasse to an ontological horizon. The multi-sensual immersion in the hyper-real haptic space is transformed into the supersensible encounter with, not a 'virtual reality', but 'the virtual' immanent in/as the real. A low-angle panning of the 3D actual forest connects with a horizontal tracking shot of the 2D painted forest depicting the legend of a tiger absorbing a man. Thus, the spatiotemporal issues of urban/rural/border areas and premodern/modern/postmodern eras give way to the dynamic between the entire civilisation and its memory inscribed in immemorial nature. In an interview, the director states that the couple in *Blissfully Yours* goes to the jungle for freedom, but is also contained within it. Far from being a prison, of course, it is more of an ontological 'zone' as in Tarkovsky's *Stalker* (1979), which confronts those who enter it with their own unconscious reverie and desire, which dissolve in an uncanny environment that debilitates their sensation and perception.

The implication of Apichatpong's bipartite structure is now clearer. In *Tropical Malady*, many connections between two parts – the couple's wandering/the search of lost love, a corpse/the dead cow, a singer/the baboon, urban noise/the sound of nature, and so forth – render the city, not separated from the jungle so much as superimposed upon it. Part 2 thus repeats Part 1, while differentiating and deterritorialising socio-historically framed reality to a latent realm in which experience is at first phenomenological, then ontological. And it is this ontological shift that makes Part 2 not just a diegetic succession from a different place, but a radical leap to a different time, the second being the pure, ghostly, legendary past that still coalesces in the present. The audacious intermission of a ten-minute blank screen precisely foreshadows this rupture: 'The time is out of joint.'

Then, what about *Syndromes and a Century*, which has no such break? The same scene of Dr Toey examining Dr Nohng opens each of the two parts slightly differently, unfolding in two forking paths that draw roughly similar maps of relationships: Part 1 consists of Toa's love for Dr Toey, who liked an orchid man, and of the homoerotic friendship between the dentist and the monk; and in Part 2, the Dr Nohng couple, and his fellow doctors. This is a cinematic fugue played between a rural hospital, the setting for Dr Toey's love triangle and a homosexual bond; and an urban hospital where a male doctor's secret love and his homosocial bond occur. Or in Buddhist terms, Part 1 is followed by Part 2, in which many things are reborn, gathering their karma. Indeed the director says that, as all those characters experience, love yields recurrent syndromes of sickness, and a century passes like a lifetime. His belief in reincarnation thus interestingly fits into the structuralist coordinate system in which the vertical axis comprises unchangeable, synchronic elements that are also aligned with the horizontal axis of diachronic narrative. Hence we have both difference and repetition.

Now the question is: when and where does the ontological turn occur in this apparently symmetrical structure? Notably, each sub-narrative often digresses rather than progresses, moving in a centrifugal rather than centripetal direction. When Dr Toey is told a fable of eclipse in Part 1, the camera pans a field that is said to have been a lake. This image-dialogue disjunction triggers our imagination of temporal strata deposited underneath, preserving the ancient moral lesson about greed and its punishment through a kind of superego: 'No matter what we do, something always watches us.' Yet when this covert gaze is visualised literally through the image of a total eclipse, it radiates the ineffable aura of a darkened sun for one time-freezing moment, the sublime event that neither human ethics nor phenomenological description could fully represent. For the image of this 'eye without a face', a black hole in the sky looks almost still and flat, just like a surrealist painting opening another world, or the tiger painting in *Tropical Malady*. But the gradual disappearance of the eclipse within the same shot implies that the transcendental realm exists as duration of immanence in the actual world. This transition from the dark 2D to bright 3D space is reversed in Part 2, when an intake vent sucking in smoke begins little by little to resemble a huge black hole which takes up most of the visual field. The immersive space of the basement then transforms itself into an immersive void that absorbs all our intellect, vision and sense. To where would we be drawn by these natural and artificial eclipses, if not to an ontological ground of the world, resonating around the Buddhist Eternal Return, Lacanian Real or Deleuzian Virtual?

Furthermore, this unfathomable image of emptiness directly cuts to the film's last scene of a too-ordinary city landscape, whose inhabitants – resting, dating, playing, doing aerobics – seem completely unaware of what lurks underground. A rupture thus exists within this single cut with no blank shot, as if to imply that the black hole, having engulfed the entire world, now belches it out. Likewise, all our everyday life may be the actualisation of the virtual at/into every moment of the present, and the realisation of an unconscious memory which we cannot even claim. This is how the supersensible becomes sensible again. Here let me call the process 'suture' in the hope of revamping this term seemingly obsolete in film studies. It can basically be viewed as the process by which that external to the symbolic field, i.e. unrepresentable difference-in-itself, is reduced to, replaced by, relativised as a single different element within the system. In brief, the unconditioned off-screen space is sutured into a shot as part of the chain of all framed shots. But no longer referring to its psycho-ideological implications, I would expand the notion to phenomenological and onto-logical dimensions, so as to ask what kind of suturing brings about our subjectivity and reality, and how its recognition extends our epistemological rather than cognitive horizon.

For example, isn't the gay communion in *Tropical Malady* a sutured form of the unrepresentable fusion of human and animal into an a-subjective state of being, whose memory is retained only among the souls of trees? In fact, love is hardly Apichatpong's theme. Love is, so to speak, a civilisational suture of an impersonal, unnamable desire and relationship between any types of being. His interest is rather the open process through which the so-called autobiographical *Syndromes and a Century* has failed to represent his recollections precisely, but succeeded in recapturing the 'feeling of the memory' while blending it with mysterious chance encounters in the present. In so doing, it becomes a Proustian reminiscence of the imaginary world where his parents – Dr Nohng and Dr Toey – re-enact what they never did as such, where they are respectively lost in the net of amorphous relationships, reincarnations, old fables and modern architecture, only to let us sense inhuman eyes viewing all human desires from an ontological ground. Far from negating love, however, the philosopher-director suggests that every love is an everyday miracle, like that monk-dentist friendship. But it is miraculous, perhaps because even more unrealised relationships underlie it; the dentist feels his dead brother reincarnated as the monk. Notable here is that this déjà-vu belongs not to his subjective memory so much as the 'unsutured' unconscious of the world itself. When we see green trees softly shining outside the dentist's clinic at night, it is rather those trees that have been watching the empty interior, recording all that transpired for the couple by day, and remaining as evidence of this remembrance as though the past is not even past. This is why the tiger in *Tropical Malady* seems to remember thousands of years' desires shared by former lives; humans becoming animals. This is why love is a human 'worldly desire' – the title of a short film by Apichatpong – that sutures the desire of the entire world as such.

Likewise, in *Syndromes and a Century*, the succession of two statue shots – Buddha and the fathers of modern Thai medicine – might imply that the Buddhist 'inter-individual' reincarnation has been sutured into the Western 'inner-individual' remediation. The natural gaze from above is sutured into a surveillance camera, whose presence is inferred by the Dr Nohng couple's alertness as they leave the hospital. And finally, we answer the question posed above: the fluorescent lamp is a sutured form of the sun! Yet not limited to the notion of civilisation suturing nature, this film also suggests that the unsutured ontological outside of civilisation still resides within its spaces, rural or urban, just as a total eclipse can take place in the underground of a modern city. Faint but persistent industrial noises fill the hospital as the ambient sound which, in turn, is sutured in the cultural form of sugar pop ballads or kitch techno rhythms. The 'white noise' of civilisation thus corresponds to the 'happy song' that nature sings. We might need systems theory or ecology to look further at how an inorganic environment is sutured into a self-organising system.

And here is the most cinematic point: it is precisely the song and image of softly rustling trees that connects the ending of *Tropical Malady* with the opening of *Syndromes and a Century*. These night and day scenes, both using low-angle long takes, show a piece of sky irised by branches and leaves, as if it were a Heideggerian 'clearing', the opening of Being. These fixed shots also evoke film history going back to the Lumière brothers. Isn't it the wind in the trees in the background, rather than the bourgeois family, that has fascinated so many cinephiles in *The Baby's Meal*? Hasn't such an index of contingent details brought cinematic notions as various as 'photogénie', 'unconscious optics', 'punctum' or 'the third meaning'? Doesn't such a fixed shot with a slight but ceaseless movement insinuate that the duration of a privileged instance, which Deleuze nearly dismisses, could become another type of 'movement-image' that might attain a Heideggerian 'boredom'? Doesn't this movement-image, then, embody Bergson's vision of everything photographing everything else – trees and the world perceiving and reacting to each other's image at every molecular moment – and his other vision of everything retaining the memory of images received and preserved, in this way possibly leaping to 'time-image'?

Just as remarkable as this fixed long take are the panning and tracking shots. Whatever object may be at centre, from a beast or ghost to calm statue or apocalyptic corridor, Apichatpong never fails to capture its surrounding aura through his steady, panoramic camera walk. Meanwhile, an ontological shift from such ecological space often occurs through the use of cut-in and zoom-in, guiding the viewer unawares to a vantage point of impersonal, inhuman gaze. In *Tropical Malady*, the camera catches the tiger in an iris-frame, and then abruptly cuts in to its persistent but impenetrable gaze. The same prolonged effect of being captivated, not stirring an inch, occurs as the camera zooms in on the ever-growing black hole in *Syndromes and a Century*. We might feel relieved when this uncomfortable encounter with the Real is finally dissolves into the peaceful mundane reality on the ground. But because of that extraordinary encounter, the closing scene with several master shots of the city, which would otherwise have looked too ordinary, now makes us ask: what on earth is this partly-serious-partly-ridiculous

Third World where everybody does aerobics to the rhythm of a kitch postmodern techno culture, trying to embody the globalised wave of well-being? It is not so easy a question, but the power of cinema lies in the ability to raise such queries, after allowing us to experience that on-screen jungle inherent to the city, in our own inner-city jungle called a cinema theatre.

In front of this screen, which drives us into a black hole then sends us back to reality, we are forced to think anew not only about image, but everything in the world. The basement of the modern hospital, the basis of our harmonious life, is still under (de)construction. And here is, if we will, a montage by Apichatpong. It connects the wind in rustling twigs with a variety of dispersed spaces, with cosmic images embedded in an immemorial fable or a high-tech architecture. This is the way that he rebuilds a new cinematic century, revisiting the memory of old cinema. Mapping and traversing this space and time preserves a cinematic experience that is rare and precious.

Apichatpong Weerasethakul: Key Films

Mysterious Object at Noon (Dokfa nai meuman) (2000): The film is unscripted and uses the 'exquisite corpse' party game as a concept, with the film crew traveling across Thailand, interviewing people and asking each person to add their own words to a story.

Blissfully Yours (Sud sanaeha) (2002): Min is an illegal Burmese immigrant living in Thailand who's contracted a mysterious rash. His girlfriend, Roong, and an older woman, Orn, take him to see a doctor. But the doctor is unable to do anything because Min is forbidden to speak, since he might reveal he is Burmese. Nonetheless, as is customary in Thai hospitals, some medicine is prescribed. Roong works in a factory, painting ceramic figurines. She feigns an illness and takes off with Min. She drives into the countryside, with the plan of having a picnic in the forest where she and Min can make love. Orn, meanwhile, is longing for love. She steals her husband's motorcycle and goes into the jungle to meet Tommy, a worker at the factory. They have sex just off the roadside, but are interrupted when the motorcycle is stolen. Tommy chases after the thief and disappears. Unsatisfied, Orn wanders deeper into the woods and stumbles upon Min and Roong, who have just finished making love.

Tropical Malady (Sud pralad) (2004): Keng a young soldier, is assigned to a post in a small city in rural Thailand. The troops' main duties, it seems, is to investigate the mysterious slaying of cattle at local farms. While in the field one day, Keng meets a country boy Tong. Later, Keng sees Tong riding in a truck in town. The two men have made a connection and embark on a romance, taking trips in the countryside. Then one night, Tong wanders off into the dark. The film's narrative abruptly shifts to a different story, about Keng sent alone into the woods to find his lost love. In the woods, the soldier encounters the spirit of a tiger shaman, who taunts and bedevils the soldier, causing him to run through the woods and become lost himself.

Syndromes and a Century (Sang sattawat) (2006): The film is a tribute to the director's parents and is divided into two parts, with the characters and dialogue in the second half essentially the same as the first, but the settings and outcome of the stories are different. The first part is set in a hospital in rural Thailand, while the second half is set in a Bangkok medical centre.

Uncle Boonmee Who Can Recall His Past Lives (Lung Bunmi Raluek Chat) (2010): This film centres on the last days of the title character. Suffering from acute kidney failure, Uncle Boonmee has chosen to spend his final days surrounded by his loved ones in the countryside. Surprisingly, the ghost of his deceased wife appears to care for him, and his long lost son returns home in non-human form. Contemplating the reasons for his illness, Boonmee treks through the jungle with his family to a mysterious hilltop cave – the birthplace of his first life. This film was winner of the Palme d'Or at Cannes in 2010 and offers many links to the films discussed in this essa; however, this study was written prior to the film's release which is why it is not directly mentioned in the main body of the text.